D1141937

and the
Language of Poetry

For my sisters, Eileen and Margaret

Seamus Heaney
and the
Language of Poetry

Bernard O'Donoghue

HARVESTER
WHEATSHEAF

New York   London   Toronto   Sydney   Tokyo   Singapore

First published 1994 by
Harvester Wheatsheaf
Campus 400, Maylands Avenue
Hemel Hempstead
Hertfordshire, HP2 7EZ
A division of
Simon & Schuster International Group

Typeset in 10/12 pt Sabon and Gill
by Keyset Composition

Printed and bound in Great Britain by
Hartnolls Limited, Bodmin, Cornwall

British Library Cataloguing in Publication Data

A catalogue record for this book is available from the
British Library

ISBN 0-7450-0716-3

---

3 4 5 6 7   01 00 99 98 97

Contents

Preface

If Seamus Heaney proves to be as important a figure in the annals of English poetry as currently seems likely, it will be because he combines with his sense of poetic mission a strong suspicion that poetry is not the most important thing in the world. This is a point he has made in a number of ways himself: in an interview with John Haffenden, he says of writing: 'there is indeed some part of me that is entirely unimpressed by the activity . . . it's the generations, I suppose, of rural ancestors – not illiterate, but not literary. They, in me, or I, through them, don't give a damn.' (Haffenden 63) In one of his greatest poems, 'A Daylight Art' from *The Haw Lantern*, he muses about art:

> Happy the man, therefore, with a natural gift
>
> for practising the right one from the start –
> poetry, say, or fishing.
>
> (HL 9)

We should remember here that the Latin *felix qui potuit* is really an impossibility trope. More recently, in a less successful but important poem in *Seeing Things*, 'Casting and Gathering', the point is made almost too explicitly:

> One sound is saying, 'You are not worth tuppence,
> But neither is anybody. Watch it! Be severe.'
> The other says, 'Go with it! Give and swerve.
> You are everything you feel beside the river.'
>
> (ST 13)

This uncertainty is what keeps his poetry alive. A prose statement of it came at the beginning of his first lecture as Oxford professor of poetry, 'The Redress of Poetry', where he says: 'Professors of poetry, apologists for it, practitioners of it, from Sir Philip Sidney to Wallace Stevens, all sooner or later have to attempt to show how poetry's existence at the level of art relates to our existence as citizens of society – how it is "of present use"', reverting to 'the Poundian phrase' of the Haffenden interview (63). This belief – that poetry has to state and justify its function if it is to be 'of present use', the classical republican ideal of *virtue* as devotion to the common good through civic participation – is an unwavering principle throughout Heaney's career. *The Government of the Tongue* debates how this civic usefulness in poetry is held in balance with the 'redressing' principle that poetry has a right to an independent existence: indeed, that it cannot perform its utilitarian civic function without its own strong and independent base. But the notion of poetry's 'present use' must be constantly borne in mind as a riposte to the Joyce revenant of 'Station Island' xii, with his decidedly unHeaneylike advice:

> You lose more of yourself than you redeem
> doing the decent thing. Keep at a tangent.
> (*SI* 93)

In this book I look at the changes in Heaney's language and his pronouncements on it in the light of this fundamental commitment to 'decency': a word in which the Latin root *decus*, 'appropriateness', is still alive, side by side with the sense of 'humaneness'. His utilitarian commitment faces some unavoidable problems in deciding on appropriate language. The principal one is to achieve clarity of utterance, something which is particularly difficult for the Irish writer working in the English poetic tradition. To be 'of present use', poetry must communicate unequivocally; at the same time it must be, in Heaney's phrase, 'faithful to its origins'. The 'generations of rural ancestors' are not just literary sceptics; they are an essential component in Heaney's poetic machinery. What happens when this language of origins is not immediately intelligible to the wider audience of English poetry?

This is not only a theoretical question. My survey of Heaney's career shows that deliberately cultivated, 'local' linguistic effects in his earlier poetry – such things as Irish metrical forms and naive, pseudo-learned diction – were misunderstood and gradually discontinued. But the abandonment of these marks of particularity, in favour of English disyllabics and clearer diction, ran the risk of losing the contact with the soil which enables poetic language to 'Antaeus-like gr[o]w strong' (in a phrase from Yeats's 'The Municipal Gallery Revisited' which has had immense general influence on Heaney). Other effects are introduced to fill the gap, and some already used are increased: local usages and pronunciations, and – most importantly – a more colloquial idiom which enables Heaney in his later poetry (inspired by Yeats's *Last Poems*) to use a daring line like the third one here:

> And lightening? One meaning of that
> Beyond the usual sense of alleviation,
> Illumination, and so on, is this . . .
> (*ST* 66)

Side by side with these changing practices, Heaney keeps up a career in criticism which is enlightening for his own poetry and for the function of poetry in general. These two things – the changes in Heaney's poetic language, and his poetic commentary – are my guiding subjects here. What I conclude from them is that Heaney believes, often reluctantly, that there are no such things as a transparent poetic medium or a poetry free of responsibility. Of his many quotable critical epigrams, the most crucial for my approach is the remark that a formal distinction is never *only* formal, 'but at once formal and also emotional'. A kind of criticism based on this insight might be termed 'political formalism'. It is something of that kind that I attempt to practise here.

Acknowledgements

Anyone writing on Seamus Heaney has to acknowledge first his unfailing courtesy and co-operation; I am especially grateful to him for letting me use a manuscript of 'Broagh' for the cover. I have been enlightened by discussions of Heaney and allied matters with – among others – John Bell, Eileen Carney, David Constantine, John Cornish, Jim Cronin, Adolphe Haberer, Hugh Haughton, Nick Havely, Marie Heaney, Mick Henry, Alan Hollinghurst, Mick Imlah, John Kelly, Jamie McKendrick, Andrew McNeillie, Dennis O'Driscoll, Tom Paulin, Barney Quinn, Stephen Regan, Dave Williams and Clair Wills. Particular acknowledgement must be made of the acute and concentrated reading of the manuscript by my wife Heather, and Andrew McNeillie; without them the book would have been even more contorted than it is. For specialist advice on the Irish language I always depend on my sister, Margaret MacCarron. In writing this book, a number of precedent writers on Heaney have been indispensable; I have been most reliant, as I think is obvious, on the work of Blake Morrison, Neil Corcoran, Alan Robinson, Henry Hart and Michael Parker. I am grateful to Jackie Jones of Harvester for commissioning the book, and for her patience with its delays. I would also like to thank Louise Wilson of the production department and Polly McGrail for her careful proof-reading. I owe an incalculable debt to my colleagues in English at Magdalen College, Oxford, John Fuller and David Norbrook – as, it goes without saying, I do to my wife and children.

ACKNOWLEDGEMENTS

I am particularly grateful to Faber & Faber for permission to quote extensively from the works of Seamus Heaney, and to Farrar, Straus and Giroux for American permissions. R. Dardis Clarke, of 21 Pleasants Street, Dublin 8, was most generous in giving permission to quote from the poetry of Austin Clarke. Finally, I am grateful to Tony Curtis for permission to use in the last chapter here some of the material from my essay on *The Government of the Tongue* in *The Art of Seamus Heaney* (3rd edn, Bridgend: Poetry Wales Press, 1994).

Magdalen College, Oxford

List of Abbreviations

1. Works by Seamus Heaney

(For bibliographical information, see p. 167.)

DD   *Door into the Dark*
DN   *Death of a Naturalist*
FW   *Field Work*
GT   *The Government of the Tongue*
HL   *The Haw Lantern*
N   *North*
P   *Preoccupations*
S   *Stations*
SA   *Sweeney Astray*
SI   *Station Island*
ST   *Seeing Things*
WO   *Wintering Out*

2. Other Works

Haffenden   *Viewpoints: Poets in Conversation with John Haffenden* (London: Faber & Faber, 1981)
YP   *Yeats's Poems*, ed. and annotated A. Norman Jeffares, with an appendix by Warwick Gould (London: Macmillan, 1989)

Introduction

'An art that knows its mind'

1. Language and Commentary

Nowadays it may need restating that language is, at least in part, not just material but a means to a definable end which can be aimed at. Heaney's poetry is always to be seen within the context 'of present use' (quoted in the Preface) that he describes in *The Redress of Poetry*;[1] it is evident throughout his writing that he is a self-conscious writer, and that his is 'an art that knows its mind' (*ST* 97). Heaney aims progressively, in the service of present usefulness, to refine his language into an appropriate form. My abiding purpose in this book is to examine the effectiveness of Heaney's language in the light of his view of poetry, and my approach is to chart chronologically the changes in that language and Heaney's commentary on it through the quarter-century from *Death of a Naturalist* in 1966 to *Seeing Things* in 1991. In its relatively brief compass, the book holds firmly to this course. Not that I believe that the language of poetry can be studied as an end in itself: the approach is founded on the belief that a sustained focus on language affords an enlightening – indeed, the most enlightening – critical approach to any writing. To follow Heaney's well-documented argument for clarity of utterance is a crucial matter, given the obvious political importance of the context in which he writes.

There is ample justification for this critical specialisation in

Heaney's many observations about the language of poetry. Since the 1970s he has repeatedly expressed anxiety about the highly personal form that criticism of his poetry was taking. For various reasons Heaney's poetry has always been examined from the viewpoint of detailed knowledge about his life. One reason is that Heaney is naturally forthcoming, and has invariably been generous with such information in giving interviews and answering queries from critics, even where it was not explicit in the poems. Another reason, no doubt, is the public nature of the events on which any Northern Irish writer draws in this era.

In any case, there is no reason for a book on Heaney at this juncture to provide biographical information, since that has been done with admirable thoroughness, especially for the period of the early and middle poetry, in Michael Parker's *Seamus Heaney: The Making of the Poet*.[2] Invaluable as such information is for an understanding of the poetry, the effect of a detailed historical/biographical bias on the criticism of it has not been entirely salutary. This criticism has tended to be interesting and informative: for example, the personal poems in *Death of a Naturalist* are obviously better understood in the light of their biographical origins.

But the personality-based criticism has become personal, in a limiting sense as well. The problem might be called the 'major–minor' issue. Already in the 1970s John Carey was saying, perhaps not without reason, 'everyone knows by now that Seamus Heaney is a major poet.'[3] Of the two most notorious recent attacks on Heaney, both home in on this adjective: Desmond Fennell[4] with directness and David Lloyd in more abstruse terminology.[5] Lloyd's attack is a particularly striking case, because having begun with a reasoned protest against what he calls the 'banal' attribution of 'major' status to Heaney, forty sophisticated pages later (in the course of which he discusses the construction of notions of nationhood in Heaney) he ends by pondering the curiosity of the recognition as the leading poet writing in English of a 'minor Irish poet': surely no less 'banal' a characterisation.

Whichever of these extremes of judgement seems more appropriate, it is obviously an unsatisfactory way to conduct a critical argument. When Heaney says of *Field Work* that he wants to speak in his own poetic voice again,[6] he is saying two things: first that the voice of the earlier poetry had been a persona; but also that that persona had been interpreted too biographically. For the critic the only way out of this impasse, at least in the short term, is to move towards a less biographical, more formalist kind of analysis, based on scrutiny of the poetry itself. The word 'formalist' is important – not to aspire to any fully worked out Jakobsonian analysis, but to make it clear that the idea of examining 'the poetry itself', rather than the conditions of its biographical production, is not a New Critical claim for placing poetry in a hermetically sealed environment, uncontaminated by non-literary circumstance. Such claims tend in practice to be even more subjective and personalised than the historical/biographical analyses.

By formalist I mean an approach founded entirely on the terms of traditional linguistic analysis. This course is justified, not only as a solution to the 'matter of opinion' dilemma, but also by the frequency of the employment of such terms in Heaney's poetry, as is illustrated abundantly below. To take a single instance here: what does Heaney mean at the end of the first poem in *Field Work* by the wish to be quickened into 'verb, pure verb'? And why does he choose that rather far-fetched metaphor to express the desire to write free of biographical cross-examination? I am not concerned to review the broad field of existing Heaney criticism, except where it impinges expressly on language. Finally, I should make it clear that I am not going to apply the more modern, metaphorical senses of the term 'language', through forced etymological analysis or the general employment of the term 'deconstructive' to mean 'questioning', except briefly in discussing *The Government of the Tongue* and *The Haw Lantern*, where a methodology like deconstruction arises in the text. A relatively impressive example of this practice is the last chapter, dealing with *The Haw Lantern*, in Henry Hart's book which, to my taste, spoils an admirably searching critical survey by the rather wooden application of such terms as 'deconstructing' (usually not in the technical Derridean sense), 'at-one-ment', 'm-other', and so on[7] (though I admire Hart's book, and conduct a running dialogue with it here). My enterprise is a more traditional one, although it will at some points converge on the techniques of formalist or political/ formalist analysis developed by such writers as Jakobson and Easthope.[8]

Of course, to define a study of any writing in this way as

primarily concerned with its language looks circular. In Mallarmé's famous formula, poems are made with words, not ideas; their language is the only access to them. But to spell out in detail what might have been taken as read is warranted in approaching Heaney's poetry, for two reasons: first, although all commentators since *Death of a Naturalist* have noted that the sensuousness of his language has been a major element in the poetry's success, there has been little sustained attempt to examine that language. I shall suggest that this is, at least in part, for the same reason that there is surprisingly little useful criticism of Yeats's language, despite universal agreement that language is of the first importance in Yeats's poetry: an uncertainty in approaching Irish-English usage.[9] This is not altogether surprising, of course: it is not to be expected that any non-standard variety of a language will be totally transparent to standard interpretation. This uncertainty is represented in Heaney's poetry by the recurrent figure of the 'stranger' or 'outsider', in such poems as 'Broagh' in *Wintering Out* and 'Making Strange' in *Station Island* (both of which are analysed at some length below).

The second reason that an examination of poetic language is particularly necessary in Heaney's case is the frequency of his express observations about language both inside and outside the poetry itself, as I have already suggested. In his celebrated essay on Hopkins, 'The Fire i' the Flint', Heaney says: 'the function of language in much modern poetry, and in much poetry admired by the moderns, is to talk about itself to itself'.[10] Hence Neil Corcoran, at first glance oddly, includes 'vocables' amongst Heaney's typical poetic subjects in a recent summary account of him.[11] This tendency to incorporate criticism in the poetry has also been noted, with disapproval, by Edna Longley in her well-known essay on *North*: 'the gap has narrowed between Heaney's creative and critical idioms, while widening between word and thing'.[12] Here I apply traditional linguistic categories (phonology, word-classes and vocabulary) in two ways: first, in an analysis of the highly characteristic kinds of language used by Heaney; second, in considering those observations about language made by him in the poetry itself. I shall bear this double perspective in mind throughout the book, and it will be my distinctive emphasis.

What the book attempts to demonstrate is that these two things

4

– the language of Heaney's poetry and the expressly linguistic terms in which he discusses it – have changed throughout his career in a series of deliberate and signalled choices. A chronological outline of these changes seems to me the most revealing path through Heaney's *œuvre*. Attention to them is crucial, too, to counter misunderstanding of Heaney's literary purposes in choosing particular styles and registers of language: for example, the calculatedly callow diction in some of the early poems ('my hitherto snubbed rodent'), or what has been misinterpreted – even by excellent readers of Heaney such as Blake Morrison – as the metrical roughness in *Death of a Naturalist* or *An Open Letter*.[13]

Heaney shows virtuosity in the employment of linguistic special effects from the outset, particularly in drawing on local usages. But the deliberateness with which they were used was often missed. It was evident from the first that Heaney *could* write with both lexical precision and metrical expertise. Indeed, formal skills are necessary to pastiche so accurately the language and style derived from Hopkins, Keats and Dylan Thomas of the pre-published poems written under the pseudonym 'Incertus'. Hart, who gives an interesting account of these poems in his second chapter, says: 'The first poems can be naive, both in craft and passion' (Hart 31); but often, even there, the craft was a deliberate working against the 'gentility principle' in the way Alvarez prescribed.[14] The choice not to employ this expertise in particular cases was clearly aiming at some other effect, an intention which is confirmed by the poet's own progressive glossing commentary on his practice. There is no more reason to believe that the metrical roughness of the early poetry is unintended than there is to believe that Heaney is unaware of the past participle of 'mow' when a character in a late poem says 'I have mowed' (*ST* 14), or that he thinks 'easier' is an adverb in 'Terminus' in *The Haw Lantern* (*HL* 5). Nobody doubts the deliberateness of the non-standard usages there. The danger arises in the more arcane departures from predictable norms, such as the classical Irish metrics, discussed in Section 5 of this introduction and at more length in Chapter 1 below, dealing with *Death of a Naturalist*.

The deliberateness of the changes in the language used is unmistakeable. For example, Seamus Deane remarked that between *North* (1975) and *Field Work* (1979) 'Heaney has taken the great risk of having shed an enabling myth after going to all the considerable trouble of making one';[15] 'make' and 'shed' are decidedly voluntary verbs. This willed change was confirmed by Heaney in his interview with John Haffenden; 'I'm certain that up to *North*, that that was one book.'[16] The external form of *North*'s myth was the 'artesian stanza', the short-lined poems that Heaney used to drill down metaphorically into his territory's and his consciousness's prehistory. The abandonment of this for a longer line in *Field Work* was an important formal choice with implications for meaning: an inextricably linked association which Heaney noted himself in the much-quoted interview confirming the willed nature of this formal shift (with James Randall in *Ploughshares*), saying: 'Of course a formal distinction is never strictly formal . . . [but] at once formal but also emotional.'[17] The choice of form has a mutual relation with choices of subject; scrutiny of the former offers revealing insights into the latter.

The authoritative source of this self-conscious reworking and choice of forms by Irish poets is clear. Yeats, who is so often the Dantesque master that Heaney follows, stated it succinctly in a famous quatrain:

> The friends that have it I do wrong
> When ever I remake a song,
> Should know what issue is at stake:
> It is myself that I remake.[18]

This argument for chosen revisions applies to all of Yeats's poetry, which, in a famous artistic statement, he said corresponded to his whole life. The same is true of Heaney, who signals his sense of vocation from the outset in 'Digging', his first poem to survive into book form. As the opening poem of his first book, it has kept its place at the start of both editions of selected poems to act as a kind of vocational dedication:

> Between my finger and my thumb
> The squat pen rests.
> I'll dig with it.
>
> (*DN* 14)

At various well-marked points in his career, Heaney pauses to take stock. An often-quoted example is 'Exposure' at the end of *North*:

> How did I end up like this?
> I often think of my friends'
> Beautiful prismatic counselling
> And the anvil brains of some who hate me
>
> As I sit weighing and weighing
> My responsible *tristia*.
>
> (*N* 72–3)

In his most recent volume, *Seeing Things*, there is a similar moment of truth when the poet reflects on

> Me waiting until I was nearly fifty
> To credit marvels.
>
> (*ST* 50)

Clearly this more transcendent, visionary poetry will require a different kind of language.

Heaney's literary device in *Seeing Things* is that the language is nearly transparent, leaving behind both the auditory weight of the material language of *Death of a Naturalist* and the more grammatically self-conscious language that he nurtured from *Field Work* onwards. *Seeing Things*, exemplified in its title-poem, is full of images of transparency that correspond to its language. Of course, transparency itself is no more than a poetic effect or ideal. Antony Easthope quotes Dryden's advocacy of 'a Plain and Natural' style in the 'Preface' to *Religio Laici* as that in which instructions for handling objects can 'be given by shewing them what they naturally are'.[19] The idea that language 'has only to avoid wordiness and it can give direct access to reality as though through a clear window' (*ibid.*) is only figurative. But the increasing employment of this figure, discarding what might be summed up as the 'wordiness' of the material diction of *Death of a Naturalist* and the elaborateness of the later grammatical metaphors, culminates in the transparent images of *Seeing Things*. In Chapter 4 below I look at that book's claims for transparency in various linguistic areas, particularly in metrical forms, phonology, vocabulary and grammar.

2. Metalanguage

The remaking of the poet traced in the passages just cited (and many others) is consistently expressed in technical linguistic terms. The reader can observe the language of the poetry changing, but the change is underlined by the poet's express commentary on it in various kinds of metalanguage. This works by the incorporation of the terms of linguistic analysis into the poems themselves, to reinforce the shifting in the kind and language chosen. And it is made particularly enlightening by changing the branch of linguistic analysis (moving between phonology, grammar and vocabulary), in keeping with the kind of function of language being given most prominence at various stages of Heaney's career.

This procedure is unusual even in the body of criticism itself in traditional practice in English, let alone in poetic texts. There is distinct unease with it even amongst critics of Heaney; an example is Derick Thomson's indignant-sounding reaction to Heaney's discussion of Auden in 'phonological and grammatical terms' in *The Government of the Tongue*.[20] I have already noted Edna Longley's unease with this narrowed gap 'between Heaney's creative and critical idioms' (Curtis 87). It is true that in Heaney this line in blurred, in keeping with his observation that a formal choice is also an emotional one. This works both ways: it is worth noting, too, when Heaney's language has been accused of sexism, that masculine/feminine is a division in grammatical gender as well as biological. But the empiricism of the English tradition enforces a sharp divide between the linguistic and the 'actual'. We are used to finding analyses of metre and diction, for example, in the practical criticism of the Richards school of New Critics which has for the most part held the field in the criticism of poetry in English against French and American pretenders. But analysis of such 'poetic' matters as metre and diction is as far as it tends to go (indeed, the word 'poetic' in English has been confined to them, which is odd by the standards of other cultures and eras). Exercises in formal criticism based on grammar and phonology – as conducted by Roman Jakobson on a Shakespeare sonnet or on Yeats, for instance,[21] – read uneasily in the English critical tradition.

Gestures towards such formal analysis have often been embarrassingly amateur, if suggestive, in the use of such imprecise terms as 'soft' and 'broad' to describe sounds. As an example we might take Thomas C. Foster's commentary on the opening lines of the most admired of the sonnets to Heaney's mother in *The Haw Lantern*:

> The cool that came off sheets just off the line
> Made me think the damp must still be in them.
> (*HL* 29)

Foster says – rightly – that the tenor is set by these lines, 'with their long run of monosyllables and their absolute regularity of scansion, iambic in the first, trochaic in the second'. But this helpful observation is followed by something much vaguer:

> Even the consonance of the *m* in the second line is understated, gentle. The Hopkinsian Heaney of *Death of a Naturalist* or the Anglo-Saxon Heaney of *North* would have stacked those consonantal chimes on top of each other – and would probably have chosen a harder phoneme in any event.[22]

I take this example because I think it *is* an enlightening linguistic approach, and that it is making exactly the right point: Heaney is making his peace with 'the tyranny of the iamb', having fought it for many years; but the metrical accuracy is undercut by Foster's phonological imprecision. Elmer Andrews, who has some aspiration towards a linguistic bent in his analysis, is even looser in his description of what is happening in the Heaney phrase which he uses as a subtitle for his book, 'All the realms of whisper':

> With the grand, cavernous sound produced by the long vowels and the *ls* and *rs* we have the womb-like mystery, closed by the resonating *m*; this slides easily, by way of the plural phoneme, into the hushed and sibilant crepitation of the last word.[23]

It is a standby of Michael Parker's practice, along the traditional I.A. Richards line. But with him, too, its impressionism presents problems: for example, he refers to 'the harsh stops "c", "k", "g" and the fricative "s"', which will not do because 'c' is not an English phoneme (Parker 106).

All criticism, of course, is ultimately impressionistic; indeed, its function is to record and rationalise literary impressions by whatever means and in whatever language it can. And there have been some effective linguistic analyses of some Heaney poems, mostly in passing: for example, by John Wilson Foster about 'Broagh' in his early essay (though I take issue with him below for failing to pick up Heaney's point about the unsayability of South Derry *gh* in regarding it as an English sound: it is an English symbol used as an inadequate approximation to represent a Gaelic sound).[24] Hart sees the crucial nature of linguistic construction: 'from the phonetic and lexical features of individual words he creates moving dramas in which religious, political, literary, and sexual differences clash and fuse' (Hart 49). Alan Robinson's brief analysis is characteristically penetrating.[25] But Heaney's poetic language, more than that of most poets, deserves more sustained attention than it has been accorded in most criticism so far, however evocative, because his use of language is always carefully weighted, and because formalist criticism of considerable sophistication occurs within the confines of the poems themselves, as well as in his criticism.

This has happened most famously in the phonological analysis of the auditory place-poems of *Wintering Out*: in 'the black O/ in *Broagh*' (*WO* 27) or the famous lines in 'Anahorish':

> *Anahorish*, soft gradient
> of consonant, vowel-meadow.
> (*WO* 16)

These passages, and others like them, have often been read as Heaney somewhat indulgently savouring the sheer sounds of words, in the impressionistic manner suggested by Andrews in the passage just quoted. Such a deduction might be drawn from an observation of Heaney's in another much-quoted interview, with Elgy Gillespie in *The Irish Times* (19 May 1972): 'I've been writing poems lately that grow out of words and ways of talking'. But the local words are always worked up into poems, with defined and controlling purposes. Heaney never indulges the taste of sounds as an end in itself; for example, the italicisation of 'Anahorish' above indicates that the word is not being savoured but being scrutinised *as* a word. The principal purpose of italics in linguistic convention is to convert a term from the realm of 'use' to that of 'mention': that is, to pause to consider its status as a sign rather than to pass through to what it signifies beyond the linguistic realm. 'Broagh' is a more clarifying example of the distinction: the poem's name refers to the place itself, in normal script; in line 9, 'the black *O/* in *Broagh*', the '*O*' and '*Broagh*' are italicised to indicate their being considered as terms rather than places (*WO* 27). I consider in Chapter 1 Heaney's own enlightening analysis of 'Broagh' in his important lecture 'Among Schoolchildren'.[26]

It is, of course, characteristic of the language of poetry to draw attention to itself in this way; indeed, formalist critics such as Jakobson make it definitive of poetic language that it 'does not disappear once it has been understood' (in Valéry's formula)[27] but continues to be present to the reader's consciousness. But there is still a crucial difference in Heaney's case. The normal situation is for literary language to draw attention to itself by various highlighting devices (the figures examined in rhetorical analysis, for example), and then to leave the reader to work with its language and meanings; Heaney rather ostentatiously stays present as a scrutiniser of the language itself: a condition described rather mind-bogglingly by Longley as 'almost incestuously involved with the contents of his own imagination' (Curtis 87).

3. Phonetic Commentary

The first striking example of this invasion of the imaginative text by linguistic terminology comes at the end of 'Broagh':

> that last
> *gh* the strangers found
> difficult to manage.
>   (*WO* 27)

The problem here is not evident on the page, and does not become so until the reader attempts to read it out loud. How are we meant to realise the italicised velar fricative? Clearly we would not say 'g, h'; but we are cautious about essaying the IPA phoneme /x/ (which is roughly what the sound is), not least because the poem says that 'strangers' find it difficult. For dialectal purposes, strangers are people other than natives of County Derry. Reactions to the poem and the issues it raises are discussed in Chapter 2 below, among the 'place-naming' poems of *Wintering Out*.

It is important, however, to realise that Heaney's primary concern here is not with the natives of County Derry and their language, but with the material language of poetry. In *The Government of the Tongue* he draws attention to 'phonetics and feelings being so intimately related in the human make-up' (*GT* 39). Throughout that book, as I argue in Chapter 5 below, Heaney is concerned with the nature and duties of lyric poetry. He tells us that he wrote these poems of place-naming with 'a great sense of release ... a joy and devil-may-careness', because they convinced him that the poet can be 'faithful to the nature of the English language ... and, at the same time, be faithful to one's own non-English origin', which for him 'is County Derry'.[28] But this is the easier part of the commentary and analysis of the language of lyric poetry (as the 'release' and 'devil-may-careness' perhaps admit); sound is the least inscrutable part of language from a material viewpoint.

So the place-name poems of *Wintering Out* proved readily amenable to demonstration of how Heaney's metalanguage worked in 'Broagh' and 'Anahorish'. The third poem of that group, 'A New Song', is equally significant as evidence of Heaney's approach to language. In this the name Derrygarve is called with evocative vagueness 'a lost potent musk', and the poem goes on to adjure 'our river tongues'

> To flood, with vowelling embrace,
> Demesnes staked out in consonants.
> (*WO* 33)

The impressionistic use of phonological analysis here (the vowels and consonants are only metaphorical) perhaps has too much of the flush of eloquence which his friend and mentor Philip Hobsbaum called 'Heaneyspeak' in some of the earlier poetry (Curtis 37). The most interesting thing is what Heaney does, and does not do, with the word 'Derrygarve'. When Yeats wrote the line 'He stood among a crowd at Dromahair',[29] the place-name was left unanalysed, simply to provide impressionistic colour as another case of 'lost potent musk'. In marked contrast to both Yeats and Heaney, John Montague uses his native place-name

Garvaghey as a calque-translation of the Irish *Garbh Faiche*, 'rough field', to provide the title of his 1972 collection *The Rough Field*.[30] Montague sacrifices the evocative 'musk' of the anglicised name Garvaghey (assuming that it is felt that it *could* convey the same impressionistic, Yeatsian euphony: obviously a matter of opinion) in order to exploit the associations of the compound name's meaning-elements to represent Northern Irish political hardship as a 'rough field': a terrain of grim historical events.

In his crucial 1977 essay 'The Sense of Place', Heaney distinguishes between this learned, etymological use of place-name by Montague and Kavanagh's less learned 'naming the actual' (*P* 142). This essay has generally been seen as a major insight into the circumstances of the modern Irish poet writing in English, but of course it is a crucial commentary on Heaney's own practice. His treatment of place-names in *Wintering Out* is interestingly balanced between Montague's learned etymologising, and Yeats's and Kavanagh's impressionistic deployment of the anglicised Irish terms. 'Broagh' and 'Anahorish' do not establish their difference from the standard by etymological scrutiny like Montague's but by phonological distancing (the '*gh* the strangers found/ difficult to manage'). It is another kind of learned practice. By contrast, 'Derrygarve' contains the same adjectival element (*garbh*: rough) as Montague's Garvaghey; the name could have had the highly suggestive translation *Rough-Oakwood*, which might serve well – or, if preferred, ironically – for the big-house tradition of novels such as John Banville's *Birchwood*. Such an analytical interpretation would have been highly appropriate for the poet who, in 'Alphabets', describes his Derry school St Columb's as 'Named for the patron saint of the oak wood' (*HL* 2).

But there is no suggestion of this kind of 'learned' interpretative translation in this case (as there is, of course, in 'Anahorish', to which Heaney provides the translating gloss 'place of clear water'. These three place-naming poems can be taken together as three clear, distinct ways of addressing the matter of linguistic fidelity to locale). In 'A New Song' Heaney follows Kavanagh in only 'naming the actual'; the etymology is submerged in language, not actually present to the user. The learning in 'A New Song' bears on the sounds of local spoken usage, in keeping with the sensuous materiality of the language. This practice is more common in Heaney than the calque-translation of 'Anahorish' because it is more in keeping with the stress he wants to place, at least at this stage, on language's actual materiality rather than its latent meaning. It is a question of whether it is the familiarity or the unfamiliarity ('difference' or 'otherness' in some modern parlances) that is being stressed.

4. Beyond the Sounds: Later Commentary

From the first, all readers commented on this materiality in Heaney's language. The source influence of that quality was variously identified as Hughes or Kavanagh, but all agreed that it was the principal element in the language of *Death of a Naturalist*. It was seen, too, as establishing Heaney as primarily a descriptive poet. Yet I think that 'descriptive' is not exactly the adjective to describe his particular brand of accuracy. We do not find in him the deictic pictorialism of, say, Chaucer or Browning or Yeats: 'The smylere with the knyf under the cloke'; or 'That's my last Duchess painted on the wall'; or 'There is grey in your hair'. It is rare in Heaney's poetry to find him just picturing in this way; what he does characteristically is to evoke through language, principally by recalling the process by which the user (usually a child) learns to assign words to experience and to choose from a verbal repertoire what the most appropriate word is (a process which is, of course, a metaphor for the poetic procedure itself). Words are found for what things feel like rather than what they look or sound like. This is a highly significant distinction for both poet and reader, because feeling is a deeper matter of interpretation than appearance or sound. A more appropriate word might be something like 'verbalisation': a process whereby experience or observation is turned into words. Heaney's fascination with this process, particularly in the child's language-learning, becomes prominent again later: in 'Alphabets' in *The Haw Lantern*, and in the return to childhood poems in *Seeing Things*.

Concern with this symbolic construction in language is the constant factor throughout Heaney's career. It needs to be spelt out, because while everyone was clear that the linguistic emphasis in the early poetry was on its sound – its most measurable physical level – it has been found more difficult to generalise about what the most prominent aspects of the language since

North have been. 'Verbalisation' as a larger term could embrace the phonological concentration of *Wintering Out* as one way of focusing attention on how language can be foregrounded. But it could also include the change in the language used (as the child grows up and its competence to assign language matures) and the different metalinguistic terminology needed to chart this development, according to whether it was phonology, grammar or vocabulary that was being considered.

From the present perspective (1994), *Wintering Out* might be seen as the end of early Heaney and *North* the beginning of his powerful middle period (as an alternative to the view that the work up to *North* is 'one book'; see p. 6 above). The predominance of its public subject in *North* means that linguistic commentary is much less common there. But there is one poem of great significance, which is concerned almost entirely with language: 'Bone Dreams'. Robert Welch[31] says that this poem is a love-poem to England; strictly, it is a love-poem to English. The linguistic commentary in it serves notice explicitly of the shift of focus from the phonological to the grammatical, at the same time as fidelity to County Derry gives way to fidelity to the English tradition – indeed, to the Anglo-Saxon poetic tradition at its most lexically characteristic in its use of the compound kenning:

> In the coffered
> riches of grammar
> and declensions,
> I found *ban-hus*.
> (*N* 28)

This poem is a fuller statement of an Irish–English division that has been present from *Wintering Out* onwards: in the Old English weak plural 'docken' in the second line of 'Broagh', for example, and more generally in the vaguer phonological opposition of consonantal English with vocalic Irish. It represents an important extension of what Heaney says about 'Broagh' in 'Among Schoolchildren'.

Wintering Out remains Heaney's most linguistically self-conscious book so far. Linguistic self-analysis is the exception in *North*, where analysis of subject is so dominant. Heaney returns to commentary with unmistakeable programmatic intent in 'Oysters', the jagged opening poem of *Field Work*. From the linguistic viewpoint, the intent is to move beyond the relatively tractable (subtle as it was) commentary of vowel, consonant and phoneme of the earlier poetry to the more ambitious metalinguistic area of grammar. The declaration comes in the aggressive closing lines of 'Oysters', with their wish to be quickened 'into verb, pure verb'. This in itself (I argue in Chapter 2 below) is an express challenge to the static language in much of *North*, betrayed by the absence of such forcefully transitive verbs as 'ate' and the proliferation of non-finite, participial constructions there ('dripping', 'inheriting', 'falling', 'imagining' in the first thirteen lines of 'Exposure', for instance). The grammatical commentary follows in later poems and criticism: for example, in these lines from 'In Illo Tempore' in *Station Island*:

> Intransitively we would assist,
> confess, receive. The verbs
> assumed us. We adored.

> And we lifted our eyes to the nouns.
> (*SI* 118)

In the event, although the poetic language of *Field Work* does move away from the static participial constructions of *North* towards more active verbal forms, the commentary is largely left undeveloped, apart from an important image in what has been thought one of the best poems in *Field Work*, 'The Harvest Bow':

> I tell and finger it like braille,
> Gleaning the unsaid off the palpable.
> (*FW* 58)

The second line here is an image of extraordinary force for the way the unverbalised can be interpreted without express eloquence: just as reading is possible without sight through braille, so understanding can be gained through tactile experience without being put into words. It is another image for a language which can be transparent without the mediation of equivocal words which introduce the possibility of misunderstanding.

The implications of this braille image (which was anticipated in 'Bog Queen' in *North*) are developed in the next declaration of commentating intent in the important first poem in *The Haw Lantern*, 'Alphabets', which shifts attention from the spoken to the written language. Before this stage, the poet has charted the child's developing understanding of how words, both as sound units ('Toome') and visual descriptions ('Thatcher'), have carried meaning. 'Alphabets' ambitiously attempts to chart the developing understanding of the language's written symbols, from 'the forked stick that they call a Y' to the metaphorical employment of written symbols, in 'the delta face of each potato pit'.

From this point onwards, Heaney's linguistic subject has often tended once again to be the child's parallel learning of language and understanding. This links strikingly with linguistic theories which propose that language and perception are coterminous: to perceive something is to assign language to it. He will claim that it was only when he was nearly fifty that he was able 'to credit marvels' (*ST* 50): to see reality unmediated, as the child does. The change of perspective is certainly linked to the child–parent relations concentrated on since the deaths of his parents and commemorated in the greatly admired series of elegies in *The Haw Lantern* and *Seeing Things*. But next in this introduction I want to go back chronologically to consider this general context of duty, particularly in relation to poetic language, and the possibility of transparent, unequivocal utterance.

5. Language and Civic Duty

At the beginning of the Preface I quoted Heaney's insistence in 'The Redress of Poetry' that the poet has to be seen as 'of present use' as a 'citizen of society'. (This should not surprise us too much: after all, Leavis said in *New Bearings in English Poetry* that all that we can fairly ask of the poet is that 'he shall show himself to have been fully alive in our time'.[32]) If the primary focus of the lyric in Heaney is increasingly on the English tradition, his focus as civic commentator is on Ireland. This is made clear in an important passage in the prefatory essay to *The Government of the Tongue*:

> In the course of this book, Mandelstam and other poets from Eastern bloc countries are often invoked. I keep returning to

them because there is something in their situation that makes them attractive to a reader whose formative experience has been largely Irish. There is an unsettled aspect to the different worlds they inhabit, and one of the challenges they face is to survive amphibiously, in the realm of 'the times' and the realm of their moral and artistic self-respect, a challenge immediately recognizable to anyone who has lived with the awful and demeaning facts of Northern Ireland's history over the last couple of decades. (*GT* xx)

Significantly, this passage is followed by an apology for the 'relative absence of Irish subjects' in the selections of writings on lyric poetry which follows. But there is no doubt that the bearing of his *public* discussions is on Ireland, and that this has repercussions for poetry, given his social conception of the poet.

Throughout his career Heaney has been greatly concerned with duty: to family, friends, politics and art. I want to concentrate here on the complex set of imperatives that have dominated his conception of himself as an Irish poet. To start once again with his Kavanaghesque notions of fidelity to the local parish: all commentators (including Heaney himself) have observed that poetry of place, often with emphasis on the phonetic form of the place-name, has been prominent in the Irish tradition as a genre called *dinnseanchas*. The term might be translated as something like 'ancient-history of places', though in modern Irish usage the second element has developed an overtone of strictly *local* history and archaeology. Pronunciation is the most evident ground of this kind of poetry, precisely because (as I said above) sound is the most materially palpable of linguistic levels.

But there is a related Irish phonological issue of great prominence in Heaney's early poetry, which has a more direct connection with the specifically literary: the question of prosody, particularly the metrical and stanzaic forms used. This placed an 'Irish subject' centrally within the poetry itself. The most notable of these was the Gaelic form *deibidhe* (discussed in some detail in Chapter 1). A stanza of the celebrated poem 'Follower' will illustrate the form which rhymes monosyllables with the unstressed syllable of a two-syllabled word:

An expert. He would set the *wing*
And fit the bright steel-pointed sock.

The sod rolled over without *breaking*.
                (*DN* 24; emphasis added)

Heaney has gradually moved away from the employment of such forms, and latterly it has disappeared, almost entirely. A later poem such as 'Lightenings' ix is in full-blown Shakespearian iambic pentameter: 'A boat that did not rock or wobble once' (*ST* 63). The arguments for and against the adoption of such Irish formalities are examined in Chapter 1. I argue there that Heaney came increasingly to see in them a kind of moral imperative that, as a writer of lyric in English with the crucial requirement of immediate intelligibility in English, he wants to feel free to resist because they introduce complexity rather than clarification by being opaque to a non-Irish readership.

However, such an inclination to resist is not the principal motivation for moving away from Gaelic metrical practice (and from the more exclusive phonological place-naming). Heaney lamented the unfeasibility of the project in a crucial interview with Edward Broadbridge in 1977:

> I have played with notions of Irishness and so on, but that's almost literary convention now, to talk about the loss of the Irish language – place-names and so on. All that's true and yet it's all over you know.[33]

Everyone quotes the occasions when Heaney makes for the open, like his Sweeney: for example, when James Joyce, in *Station Island*, urges him not to lose himself 'doing the decent thing' but to 'fill the element/ with signatures on your own frequency' (*SI* 94: the auditory image is significant). But Heaney's concern for the perspicuity of the poetic medium is a more significant constraint. To use alienating dialect may be an accurate image of difference, but it conflicts with another imperative which is the most compelling of all for a writer who wishes to clarify the medium. This point is made expressly and repeatedly throughout the corpus, for example in the famous closing lines of the poem 'North':

> 'Keep your eye clear
> as the bleb of the icicle,
> trust the feel of what nubbed treasure
> your hands have known.'
>   (*N* 20)

The bleb of the icicle represents perfectly the transparency of the medium, as a balancing contrast to language's material opacity.

The last chapter of this book is an examination of *The Government of the Tongue*, Heaney's *ars poetica* which outlines his theory of lyric poetry and its forms, especially in relation to two dominating authorities, Dante and Mandelstam. This theory belongs in a well-established tradition of the lyric's ambitions towards direct, 'natural' utterance. Heaney quotes repeatedly Lowell's formulation of it in 'Epilogue' (in the 'South Bank Show' interview with Melvyn Bragg, for instance):[34] 'Yet why not say what happened'?[35] The problem for the poet setting out to 'say what happened' is a matter of language: of how to achieve the ideal speaker–hearer relationship, in Chomsky's terms. To be faithful in saying what happened in the parish will require parochial terms, such as the dialect forms used in *Death of a Naturalist*. This dilemma – it is almost a paradox for the writer who wishes their meaning to be unequivocal – is discussed at some length in Chapter 5 below in describing Heaney's view of Dante as a writer rooted in place. The problem is how to verbalise those happenings in a way that will be directly and clearly intelligible to the 'stranger' reader. It is a problem of translation.

There is a further paradox: the more urgent the message to be expressed, the more transparent the language must be. This is paradoxical because Heaney's urgencies tend to be Irish ones; but the unfamiliar Irish forms are not the clearest way to encapsulate them. Hence the evocative verbalisations of *Death of a Naturalist* will not meet the requirements of *North*. The success of Heaney's change of language by *North* found its most eloquent testimony in Conor Cruise O'Brien's well-known remark about the transparency of that volume's language: 'I had the uncanny feeling, reading these poems, of listening to the thing itself',[36] echoed by Blake Morrison's (somewhat less approving) observation of the 'several points in *North* where one feels that Heaney is not writing his poems but having them written for him, his frieze composed almost in spite of him by the "anonymities" of race and religion' (Morrison 68).

The achievement of such a language clearly involves the abandonment of the various highlighting devices which constituted an important part of the appeal of the early poetry, such as the evocative dialect usages and the Irish metrical forms. Once the constricted, accurate language has served its purpose, the poet declares his wish (noted above) to move back to a more expansive kind of writing, in his abandonment in turn of the myth of *North*. But the creative tension between the wish to be faithful to origin and the wish to aspire to transparency in lyric utterance remains constant in Heaney's writings and deliberations.

6. Middle Voices

Side by side with the increasing employment of the more 'normal' English metrical form, iambics, Heaney maintains the fidelity to County Derry claimed for the place-name poems by other, more transparent means. Hence we witness the child's language-learning all over again, but now often with an outsider's (such as a grown-up's) perspective on it. The local forms in the later poetry are mostly idiomatic usages which express the gap between local and standard language from a more knowing, learned perspective by a kind of Joycean parallax. Here the programmatic poem is *Station Island*'s 'Making Strange', the title of which is itself metalinguistic: a version of Russian Formalist defamiliarisation, put to wonderfully quotidian purpose. The poet introduces a stranger 'with his travelled intelligence' to 'another', a local 'unshorn and bewildered/ in the tubs of his wellingtons'. 'A cunning middle voice' intervenes, telling the poet to 'Be adept and be dialect', providing a whole new set of linguistic possibilities which are, of course, also continuous from his previous practice:

> I found myself driving the stranger
>
> through my own country, adept
> at dialect, reciting my pride
> in all that I knew, that began to make strange
> at that same recitation.
>
> (*SI* 32–3)

The operative term here is the 'middle voice'. In *The Government of the Tongue*, Heaney uses it twice in a more grammatical way (though still in nothing like the technical sense of the Greek or Icelandic verb's middle voice): he says that part of Lowell's 'Ulysses and Circe' is 'spoken in a middle voice' (*GT* 143), and in the discussion of Auden he remarks significantly: 'the grammatical peace of this present participle is disturbed by a lurking middle voice: the grass is chafing, active, but in so far as the only thing being chafed is itself, it is passive' (GT 123). I consider this use of the verb in Heaney's own poetry in the course of the discussion of *North* below, arguing that it is to be seen as another figure for the 'whatever you say, say nothing' dilemma. It is a language balanced between (in Corcoran's terms) the 'static nouns of earth' and the quickened 'pure verb'.[37] In that chapter I propose a verbal 'chain of being' which is remarkably consistent across all Heaney's writings, extending from active and transitive verbs at the top, associated with free poetic utterance, to the solid, immovable nouns at the bottom, linked to dominant obligation, whether political, historical, or (in 'In Illo Tempore': *SI* 118) religious.

In the metalinguistic employment of the term middle voice in 'Making Strange', there is no connection at all with the grammatical middle voice of the verb, beyond the metaphorical. But it is typical of the way Heaney makes grammatical categories repay their debt to the language. It is the latest metaphorical employment of linguistic terminology, following on from the vowel/consonant, 'all verb', transitive/intransitive, and so on. This linguistic location halfway between the local and the learned (between Kavanagh and Montague again) has proved to be an enormously rich vein, from the haunting dialectal grammar in sonnet 4 ('Clearances') in *The Haw Lantern* ('You/ Know all them things') to the subtle misrepetition of the past participle in 'Man and Boy' in *Seeing Things*:

> He has mown himself to the centre of the field;
>
> 'I have it mowed as clean as a new sixpence'.
>
> (*ST* 14)

The dialectal strength is not patronised, and at least holds its own; it becomes part of the official poetic voice in 'Terminus': 'Two buckets were easier carried than one' (*HL* 5), and it is related to the colloquial 'and so on' of the important definitive poem xii at the end of 'Lightenings' (*ST* 66).

This 'middle voice' is the most interesting pretension so far to a neutral language (in the same sense in which iambic pentameter is the normal, 'unmarked' metre for English), enabling the poet to claim that the language of *Seeing Things* is indeed a transparent medium with access to the transcendent. This chimerical ideal is the culmination to date of Heaney's move away from the inescapably palpable, material language of *Death of a Naturalist*. Yet it manages to be no less locally founded than that dialect of the early poetry with its 'Tractors hitched to buckrakes' (*FW* 15). His language has reached the point prophesied by Hobsbaum in that essay on *Wintering Out*: 'What the critics of our day acclaim as achievement, those of the future may very well look back upon as promise' (Curtis 43).

Although this book consistently takes language as the point of access to Heaney's work throughout his career, it is not narrowly philological. Neither is it couched in rhetorical terms, as it could have been: for example, Section II of 'A Retrospect' in *Seeing Things* might have been analysed in terms of oxymoron, and its implications developed; 'Settings' xxii (*ST* 78: the 'set questions for the ghost of W.B.' – questions, incidentally, that Heaney answers better than Yeats) is a run of rhetorical questions (*ST* 78), another favoured Heaney device. But my concern is with the development of Heaney's interests and subjects in their public contexts, and how his changing use of language responds in turn to those developments. Accordingly, I begin with a consideration of what seems to me to be the starting-point for Heaney: his relation to the Irish poetic tradition, especially to Robert Farren's account of Larminie's proposal for a distinctively Irish metrics in English.[38] That sounds recherché, but I think it is central to the kind of decision Heaney (or, indeed, any Irish poet) had to make in choosing the form for his concerns. As Heaney says, forms do not occur by nature: they have to be chosen; sometimes they have to be changed, according to the work they are required to do. From the first chapter the book proceeds chronologically through the nine major volumes of poetry, before concluding with an examination of Heaney's *ars poetica*. Naturally, I have drawn attention to the shifts in the poet's choices: the movement from what Eliot on Milton called 'the hypertrophy of the auditory imagination'[39] (a dominant critical phrase for Heaney, as discussed in the Auden essay in *The Government of the Tongue*) towards a more transparent, limpid language in *Seeing Things*. But despite this inevitable emphasis on changes, I hope that what principally emerges from these pages is a sense of what is consistently present in a writer whom I believe to be the most expert and considered practitioner of English poetry in our time.

1

English or Irish Lyric? (1960s Heaney)

As I suggested in the Introduction, few poets signal the choices they are making at every juncture as explicitly as Heaney does: the choice between confinement to Irish subjects or not; between the Irish and English poetic traditions; or between political responsibility – the 'responsible *tristia*' of 'Exposure' – and artistic freedom. Most of the criticism of Heaney to date has been devoted to the last of these. Morrison (1982), Corcoran (1986), Andrews (1988) and Tamplin (1989),[1] in their chronological accounts, have all given central consideration to the arts–politics divide, as have the most celebrated shorter discussions of Heaney, such as those of Carson or Longley (in Curtis, 1985), and inevitably it is a major concern of the biographical critics like Parker (1993). That this emphasis is well placed is unquestionable; the obligation or otherwise of public answerability is one of the most addressed poetic questions of our time, as predicted in the Introduction to the Motion–Morrison Penguin anthology.[2]

The principal concern of this chapter will be with the second choice here: between the Irish and English poetic traditions. Irish poets are very aware of this: unduly so, according to a number of authorities, such as Dillon Johnston and Edna Longley who warns that Ireland is not a good staple diet for the Irish writer.

In 1974 Robert Lowell famously called Heaney 'the best Irish poet since Yeats'. Apart from the evaluation here, another question arises: what exactly is meant by 'an Irish poet'? A poet who is Irish, irrespective of what he writes? A poet who writes in the Irish language? Or a poet committed to writing with an awareness of a precedent Irish poetic tradition? Is 'Irish poet' the most helpful way to characterise Heaney? Heaney's bardic credentials were questioned in a curious way in 1991, in relation to the seventy-fifth anniversary of the Dublin Easter Rising, by Desmond Fennell, who observed: 'Heaney is not being an "Irish poet" all the time'.[3] What Fennell demands is that the Irish poet should be concerned at all times with Irish matters.

This question of definition is not something to which Heaney himself would be indifferent. He has always been greatly concerned to recognise his influences, the predecessors and traditions that have made him what he is. His model of literary tradition is Eliot's 'Tradition and the Individual Talent',[4] which says all writers have to balance individuality with an informed sense of the tradition they are writing in. In an important essay on Heaney, Neil Corcoran takes note of this dilemma: 'as a poet who considers himself Irish, Heaney lies at an oblique angle to the English poetic tradition, and must labour to create his own personally sustaining "tradition" of sought-out exemplars'.[5] Several of the essays in *Preoccupations* reflect this concern with example and placing: as has often been noted (in that same Corcoran essay, for instance), the essay 'Yeats as an Example?' (*P* 98–114) appends a question mark to the title of an essay by Auden, indicating uncertainty about his relationship to the major Anglo-Irish poet.

The question of where Heaney placed himself as a poet arose most celebratedly in his reaction to the location of him in Motion–Morrison's *The Penguin Book of Contemporary British Poetry* (1982). Heaney's *An Open Letter* ended by declaring the poet's reluctance 'to bite/ Hands that led me to the limelight/ In the Penguin book'[6] in rejecting his categorisation as a British poet. His reluctance was all the greater because one of the editors was his 'good advocate' (stanza 8) Blake Morrison, who wrote the first authoritative book-length study of Heaney in the same year as the anthology was published. And it is not surprising that the genial Heaney was reluctant to bite the hand (in Edmund Burke's phrase), considering this accolade from the anthology's Introduction:

There is another reason why British poetry has taken forms quite other than those promoted by Alvarez [in the essay prefixed to his 1962 anthology *The New Poetry*]: the emergence and example of Seamus Heaney. The most important new poet in the last fifteen years, and the one we very deliberately put first in our anthology, Heaney is someone Alvarez could not foresee at the time . . .[7]

Readers responded variously to Heaney's cautious reaction to this handsome recognition, some feeling it to be surprisingly churlish. But this would be trivialising, even if it were true; editors have mostly been sensitive to the difference between 'British' and 'Irish' affiliation, sometimes risking clumsiness rather than lose precision in the titles used to distinguish them. For example, Michael Schmidt's 1983 anthology was unaphoristically named *Some Contemporary Poets of Britain and Ireland*, even though the only Irish representatives there were Mahon and Paulin, both of them Belfast Protestants of 'British' heritage. Besides, it was hard to ignore the comment I have quoted above: that Heaney was a 'reason why *British* poetry has taken the forms' it has. Most of the several Irish poets included in the anthology felt some unease with the 'British' heading, and it was appropriate (and courageous) for their most highly praised representative to make the point. As Heaney says in the *Open Letter*, there had been a series of similarly entitled 'British' anthologies featuring Irish poets; rather than to 'let it go' (stanza 5), he takes this as a suitable occasion to register his demurral by addressing his most sympathetic anthologists in the genial medium of the Burns stanza, which has a disarming friendliness to it. It has frequently been used for epistolary friendliness and respect – in Auden's 'Letter to Lord Byron', for instance, or John Fuller's *Epistles to Several Persons*.[8]

So there was plenty of reason for Heaney to register his mild caveat, which was further disarmed by its deliberate roughness of rhyme in a form marked for its virtuoso urbanity (though I note below how this calculated peasant roughness was surprisingly misunderstood). But there was a further reason why Heaney might have felt that he could not opt for a quiet life and settle for the editors' praise. As far as the content of his poetry is concerned, he could have 'let it go': it was hardly necessary for the poet of *North* to remind us that his 'passport 's green'. What I want to suggest here is that Heaney might have been glad of an opportunity to declare himself an Irish poet, given his increasing tendency to avoid another well-turned Irish furrow which it has been obstinately difficult for the Irish poet to ignore: the employment of distinctively Irish poetic forms.

Heaney's connection with the formalities of Irish poetry in Irish is recognised as important in the introduction to the section on 'Contemporary Irish Poetry' in *The Field Day Anthology of Irish Writing*[9] by Declan Kiberd, who notes:

> a surprising number of elements from the Gaelic tradition may be found in modern poetry, especially that of Heaney, who has taken on an almost bardic aura. . . .Among the duties of the ancient bards was *dinnseanchas*, knowledge of the lore of place.

Heaney's use of *dinnseanchas* is described in Chapter 2 below, in discussing the place-name poems in *Wintering Out*. At the end of the Introduction I noted his apology to that Irish tradition for representing it so little in the pages of *The Government of the Tongue*, as well as his regretful observation to Edward Broadbridge in 1977 that the 'notions of Irishness' and 'the loss of the Irish language' are 'all over'.[10] Yeats – never far from Heaney's mind in the matter of canonical descent – voices some anxiety in the matter, saying in 'A General Introduction for My Work': 'Gaelic is my national language, but it is not my mother tongue'.[11]

Irish is not Heaney's mother tongue either, but he knows it very well, and he has always been actively interested in Irish-language poetry. As late as 1983 (the same year as *An Open Letter*), in the John Malone lecture in Belfast, 'Among Schoolchildren',[12] Heaney translates a poem from Seán Ó Riordáin's Irish as 'Come Back Again', including these lines:

> Unshackle your mind
> Of its civil English tackling,
> Shelley, Keats and Shakespeare.
> Get back to what is your own.
> Wash your mind and wash your tongue
> That was spancelled in a syntax
> Putting you out of step with yourself.

It is only a translation, of course, not a manifesto; but it at least indicates a strong awareness of the poet's connections with a pre-English, Irish poetic tradition.

But a consciousness of Irish poetic forms has been unignorable since the end of the last century for all Irish poets writing in English, even if they lacked the reputation Kiberd attributes to Heaney. Yeats's anxious admission of his lack of Irish betrays an insecurity that has hag-ridden Irish poets since the nineteenth-century Celtic revivalists, especially after the founding of the Gaelic League in the 1890s. Even if the writers thought that actually learning the language was going a bit far (thus George Moore said he was too old to learn it himself, but made it a condition in his will that his niece and nephew should learn Irish before inheriting his estates), the idea gained currency that it is possible, or even obligatory, for Irish poets writing in English to incorporate elements of the Irish language into their poetic practice. The most promising area to draw upon was thought to be metrics and other such technicalities of poetics.

The history of this attempt is quite a familiar one, but it warrants retelling for its important bearing on Heaney's poetry. The minor nineteenth-century Irish poet William Larminie is much more famous, as Robert Farren said,[13] for what he proposed in passing than for his own writings. In 'The Development of English Metres' (*Contemporary Review*, 66, November 1894), at the end of a largely negative survey of modern metrical habits in English, Larminie suggested that assonance drawn from the practice of Gaelic Irish poetry could be used in English by Irish poets, noting, for example, that in Old Irish assonance of consonants, as well as of vowels, was significant. His much-quoted conclusion says:

> Irish writers would certainly have left their mark in English literature should they be found to have taken a conspicuous part in the creation of a body of metres having in them the promise of the future, rich with unexhausted possibilities. (Farren 5)

This heady idea roused Yeats and (especially) AE to a frenzy of enthusiasm. Indeed, it has continued to inspire at least a wistfulness in many Irish poets, from Stephens to Austin Clarke to Paul Muldoon, ever since. In 1951 Clarke still reports that 'AE kept reminding us constantly of Larminie's theory' for many years afterwards.[14]

There were other tendencies in this direction. Elsewhere in the same book, Clarke says that Yeats and AE were inspired in their own metrical practice by Ferguson's 'Fairy Thorn', with its 'vowel-music suggested by Gaelic internal assonance' (Clarke 15). Robert Welch claims that 'Hyde's translations ... (especially those in the *Love Songs* [of Connacht]) had a profound effect on the course of Irish verse in English in the 1890's and well beyond, and this in both letter and spirit.'[15]

For the most part, it was evident from the first that the attempt to reproduce exactly the formalities of Old Irish metre in English were unlikely to succeed. Indeed, it was far from clear what this notional project would mean in practice. What, for example, does Yeats mean, precisely, when he says: 'If somebody could make a style which would not be an English style and yet would be musical and full of colour, many others would catch fire from him, and we would have a really great school of ballad poetry in Ireland'?[16] He is not just referring to the literal replacement of Mediterranean Blue by Irish colours, or to drawing on 'the fountain of Gaelic legends', interested as he was in both things. He means 'the verses and stories that the people make for themselves'.[17] But – more interestingly – he is also claiming that what he, Lionel Johnson and Katherine Tynan were engaged upon was to make 'a more subtle rhythm, a more organic form, than that of older Irish poets who wrote in English'.

The attractions of this chimerical scheme of drawing on classical Irish technicalities to achieve some subtler or richer rhythm in English were enhanced by its successes in modified application. The best discussion of the matter comes in Study 6, 'The Irish Mode', in Thomas MacDonagh's *Literature in Ireland*.[18] MacDonagh demonstrates intriguingly that some of the practices of Gaelic metrics and syllabics were practised by writers of Yeats's generation. For example, he considers the First Musician's songs from Yeats's *Deirdre*:

> 'Why is it', Queen Edain said,
> 'If I do but climb the stair
> To the tower overhead,
> When the winds are calling there,

Or the gannets calling out
   In waste places of the sky,
There's so much to think about
   That I cry, that I cry?'[19]

MacDonagh comments:

> This poem is really syllabic, seven syllables to the line, like one
> species of *Deibidhe* poems in Irish – without, of course, the
> arrangements of assonance. I do not know if Mr Yeats is aware
> of this syllabic measure; but again and again in his poems and in
> the poems of many contemporary Irishmen I find this tendency.
> (MacDonagh 72)

MacDonagh then gives an excellent explanation of the distinctions
between quantitative and accentual/stressed metres: Irish, like
English, is primarily accentual, but

> there is this occasional difference, that while what may be called
> central English verse, in order to emphasize the stressed,
> underemphasizes the unstressed, Irish frequently allows for the
> clear pronunciation of several syllables between stress and stress

– giving as an example Yeats's 'The Lake Isle of Innisfree': 'And I
shall have some peace there, for peace comes dropping slow'. The
point is borne out by Yeats's celebrated reading of this when he
emphasises all syllables of the first seven (that is, the *deibidhe* line)
equally, including the concluding 'there', which would have very
slight emphasis in an English reading that would give a stress to 'I'
and 'peace', submerging the other syllables. There are, as MacDo-
nagh says, other prominent aspects of the Old Irish system that
are not consistently represented (of which the full and complex
assonantal system is the most important), but it is hardly
coincidental that in at least two respects Yeats's practice here does
conform to the system.

One other detail of *deibidhe* practice might be noted; it is the
favourite detail of poets from Austin Clarke to Muldoon, and I
shall be making a good deal of it in the pages which follow. This
is the elegant, but initially very rough and un-English, rhyming of
a monosyllable with a disyllable stressed on a syllable other than
the rhyming one. This practice, too, is curiously paralleled in

Yeats – for example, in the half-rhymes which Stan Smith quotes from him, without reference to the Irish tradition: 'distress' with 'clumsiness' in 'A Dialogue of Self and Soul', for example[20]. Two stanzas of Clarke's fine translation of the seventeenth-century poem 'Beatha an Scoláire' ('The Scholar's Life') illustrate the practice (emphasis added):

> Paying no dues to the parish,
> He argues in *logic*
> And has no care of cattle
> But a satchel and *stick*.
>
> The showery airs grow softer,
> He profits from his *ploughland*
> For the share of the schoolmen
> Is a pen in *hand*.[21]

A successful example which illustrates the appeal of these technical adaptations is Clarke's best-loved poem, 'The Planter's Daughter':

> When night stirred at sea
> And the fire brought a crowd in,
> They say that her beauty
> Was music in mouth
> And few in the candlelight
> Thought her too proud,
> For the house of the planter
> Is known by the trees.
>
> Men that had seen her
> Drank deep and were silent,
> The women were speaking
> Wherever she went –
> As a bell that is rung
> Or a wonder told shyly,
> And O she was the Sunday
> In every week.[22]

Although not all the success of this great lyric poem can be assigned to Irish metrical sources, some of it certainly can, such as the basic seven-syllable line (lines 2, 5, 7, 14, 15) and the steadily trisyllabic 'every' in the last line, which illustrates MacDonagh's

point about the prominence of unstressed syllables. Most sig-
nificantly, the poem's crowning lyrical glory – the 'O' in the
penultimate line – converts a pat six-syllable dactylic line to the
deibidhe's more rough-hewn heptasyllabic. More obviously, the
assonantal recurrences are typical of classical Irish poetry: the 'au'
diphthong in 'crowd', 'mouth', 'proud'; and the 'i:' vowel in
'seen', 'deep', 'speaking' and 'week'.

To demonstrate the truth of Clarke's and Welch's claim that
Larminie's principles have survived, here is the start of Paul
Muldoon's 'Why Brownlee Left' (another candidate for a small
anthology of the best Irish lyrics in English):

> Why Brownlee left, and where he went
> Is a mystery even now.
> For if a man should have been content
> It was him. . .[23]

Much of Muldoon's brilliant loose rhyming throughout his work
could be seen as a variant on Old Irish patterns, in the same way
that many of the lines of 'Why Brownlee Left' seem to be
variations on the *deibidhe*'s seven-syllable line ('By noon Brownlee
was famous'). Muldoon's general indebtedness to Clarke seems to
me to have been underrecognised; but that is another story.

But this is an area of great difficulty for the critic. These
semi-osmotic influences can be either ignored (a wise course) or
guessed at. The latter strategy is very risky. Three examples might
be cited to show this. In *The Language of Irish Literature*, Loreto
Todd chances her arm here: 'Irish poets continue to be influenced
by Gaelic rhythms and sound patterns and continue to absorb the
oral traditions, because these have been transformed into a unique
form of English,'[24] This is not proving very much; Todd goes on
to say, even less convincingly: 'MacNeice emulates Yeats's inter-
nal rhyme and extended assonance',[25] with the vague suggestion
that there is something Old Irish about it all. Colin Meir, in *The
Ballads and Songs of W.B. Yeats*,[26] attributes a number of
Yeatsian effects – all of them, in fact, peculiarities of the poet's
own practice, and arguably attributable to the archaising tradition
of English poetic diction – to Hiberno-English influence: for
example, the alliterating 'drinks his drop' ('A Dialogue of Self and
Soul'); the participle in 'What need you, being come to sense'

('September 1913'); and Yeats's own deictic tendency to use the demonstrative 'that' in unidiomatic ways ('that William Blake/ Who beat upon a wall'[27]). None of these is a real feature of Irish spoken usage.

A last example of this understandable but inaccurate guessing, one which is closer to the metrical discussion here, shows the even greater difficulty that used to be encountered in approaching poetic phonology. In *The Lonely Tower*[28] (113, n. 2) T.R. Henn quotes these lines from Yeats's early 'Lullaby', inviting us to 'note the extreme subtlety of the vowel tones; there are at least four separate values of the *o*- sound:

> Sleep, beloved, such a sleep
> As did that wild Tristan know
> When, the potion's work being done,
> Roe could run or doe could leap
> Under oak or beechen bough,
> Roe could leap or doe could run'.[29]

It is not quite clear what Henn means; but all these *o* -sounds are not tonal variants but the same /ou/ diphthong. We might compare this with the uncertainty that has resulted when Heaney commentators have had recourse to impressionistic phonetics, described in Section 2 of the Introduction above.

The enterprise of writing or interpreting the prosodic effects of one language or dialect in another is a dangerous one, as all these experiences suggest. The reason for this has been stated authoritatively by Paul Fussell Jr, discussing the possibility of replicating the devices of Old English metre in modern English:

> For although Old English verse can be recalled and imitated (as in Auden's *Age of Anxiety*), nothing really like it can be recovered; the language has changed, and each significant linguistic change projects us into an altered prosodic world in which the meters of the past can perhaps be understood but never again commonly practiced.[30]

This clearly has enormous implications for a major point of dispute within Irish poetry: Thomas Kinsella's contention – greeted with unbridled rage by some reviewers, such as Conor Cruise O'Brien – that Irish literature offers the extraordinary case of a poetry which survives a change of vernacular, from Irish to English.[31] The conclusions from Fussell's argument would be that this makes little sense, attractive a notion as it has proved to be for some Irish poets.

It is not surprising that Heaney was attracted by this idea of rich phonetic coloration, given his observations about the closeness of phonetics and feeling (*GT* 39). Such notions of the independence of the auditory imagination remain an issue for him up to the Auden essay in *The Government of the Tongue*, well after he has ceased to use Irish metrical devices. But even well-disposed non-Irish readers tended to misread stylistic effects taken from Irish (as I show immediately below), and this may have been a factor in his gradual, reluctant abandonment of them. Heaney's involvement with Irish-derived metrical schemes has become increasingly slight, though both his practice and his commentary have shown a marked inclination towards them from the first.

Despite the appeal of the occasional, decorative *deibidhe* rhyme, Heaney's resistance to Larminie's assonantal project is stated forcefully in the famous interview with Seamus Deane in the first issue of *Crane Bag*, confirming what he said to Broadbridge, also in 1977: 'Discussion of what tradition means has moved from a sort of linguistic nostalgia, a puerile discourse about assonance, metres and so on, to a consideration of the politics and anthropology of our condition.'[32]

But that was in 1977. For the kind of poet Heaney was in *Death of a Naturalist* – of rural Irish origins, writing of matters deeply rooted in Irish experience – the desire for such a 'puerile discourse', traditional from Larminie and Hyde to Clarke, did hold great appeal. And sure enough, we find marked *deibidhe* effects in some of the early poems, as in 'Follower':

> An expert. He would set the wing
> And fit the bright steel-pointed sock.
> The sod rolled over without breaking . . .
>
> I wanted to grow up and plough,
> To close one eye, stiffen my arm.
> All I ever did was follow . . .
>
> (*DN* 24)

'Wing/breaking' and 'plough/follow' are clearly *deibhidhe* rhymes. But it is striking that the metrical 'home key' even here is the English octosyllabic, not the Irish seven-syllable line. Even the first line, which does feature the level stressing of the Irish practice to achieve a metrical suppleness, has eight syllables: 'My father worked with a horse plough' (*DN* 24).

In the later *Crane Bag* interview, Heaney also recognised the difficulties, saying of the Northern Irish writers: 'Though harking to different writers all of us in this group were harking to writers from the English cultural background.'[33] Accordingly, it was understandable that good readers of Heaney – such as Blake Morrison, or Roland Mathias in Curtis's *The Art of Seamus Heaney* – mistakenly diagnosed a metrical roughness here which is ironed out later on. What they experienced as roughness *does* become uncommon later; but at this stage it is calculated. We can be confident that it was deliberate because Heaney himself recalls Philip Hobsbaum, the mentor of the Belfast 'Group', urging the young writers, including Heaney, to 'roughen' the diction. He tells us that Hobsbaum 'emanated . . . trust in the parochial, the inept, the unprinted' (*P* 29); Hobsbaum expressed the opinion that Heaney was at first overinclined to metrical smoothness (Curtis 40). But the deliberateness of Heaney's roughening Irish effects might be missed because they were placed in an essentially smooth quantitative, rather than accentual, metrical context. And even though there are common recurrences of these rhyme patterns throughout Heaney's poetic career (to take an example more or less at random, 'homesick/stick' from 'The Harvest Bow' in *Field Work*), English patterns, especially that of Shakespearian blank verse, become increasingly dominant.

A ready example might be taken from one of the best of the marvellous twelve-line poems in *Seeing Things*:

> The annals say: when the monks of Clonmacnoise
> Were all at prayers inside the oratory
> A ship appeared above them in the air.
>
> (*ST* 62)

This is not only generally reminiscent of blank verse; it sounds, more particularly, like this famous passage from Coriolanus's defiant late speech:

If you have writ your annals true, 'tis there,
That, like an eagle in a dovecote, I
Fluttered your Volscians in Corioles.[34]

At the risk of labouring the parallel, the second line of the
Coriolanus quotation is closely paralleled in its tripartite structure
by a later line in Heaney's poem: 'The abbot said, "unless we help
him". So . . .'. Heaney is following the mainstream of English
metrics in being responsive to Shakespearian blank verse as the
principal metrical form. But he has escaped the ghost of Larminie.

This might seem a sensible enough thing to do, in the light of
Fussell's reservations quoted above about the impossibility of
reproducing the prosody of one language in another. But I do not
think this is why Heaney does it. The subject matter of his poetry,
after all, does not show him to be especially anxious to conform
to English traditions. At least once he voices something like
resentment at the dominance of English lyric form:

> Ulster was British, but with no rights on
> The English lyric.
> ('The Ministry of Fear', *N* 65)

What I want to propose here is something of a paradox: that it is
precisely Heaney's anxiety to 'say what happened', to 'pray for the
grace of accuracy', that leads him to use the normative patterns of
the English lyric in his own English language lyrics. The phrases
just quoted come from Lowell's poem 'Epilogue' in *Day by Day*,[35]
a poem mentioned already which has been central to Heaney's
enterprise since its appearance in 1977, because it encapsulates
what was his objective from the first. He has referred to it
repeatedly: recently in the 'South Bank Show' interview with
Melvyn Bragg. The use of a transparent, less attention-seeking
medium than Clarke's assonantal Celtic-Romanesque lends itself
better to a direct confrontation with 'the politics and anthropolo-
gy of our condition'. In the Yeats essay, Heaney quotes these lines
from Lowell's 'Epilogue', and adds: '"Accuracy" seems a modest
aim, even when it is as richly managed as it is here' (*P* 99). But it
is increasingly evident throughout Heaney's poetic career that
accuracy is *not* a modest aim, and is far from easily achieved; the
aspiration towards it remains an aesthetic ideal. One of the means

used to declare this ideal was the increasing choice of formal structures whose familiarity provides an ostensibly transparent medium of expression.

But this fidelity to the norms of English poetics comes only gradually. Throughout his career Heaney displays a Bloomian anxiety about his relation to the native Irish poetic tradition, as he moves farther away from the practices laid down in the 1890s by writers of the Celtic revival such as Larminie and Hyde. One of the virtues of Michael Parker's scrupulous chronological study is the prominence it accords to Heaney's reading of Daniel Corkery's *The Hidden Ireland* in his early writing. We also learn from Parker that Heaney's interest in Corkery had some depth; he lectured on him at the 1964 Belfast Festival of the Arts (Parker 58). Corkery's book, published in 1924, had reinforced the aspirations of the Celtic revivalists with examples of Irish poetry, bringing its formal devices such as hendecasyllables and *deibidhe* rhymes into English. To quote again from 'The Scholar Life', now in Corkery's translation:

> Early rising, shepherding . . .

> Great the harvest of his plough
> Coming in the front of spring.[36]
> (Corkery 79)

Certain aspects of the traditional practice are markedly manifest in Heaney's early work, such as the *deibidhe* rhymes from 'Follower' quoted above, though even there the rhymes were contained in a strongly iambic metre. The use of this as a decorative effect, in the same way that Victorian writers used a loose alliteration, persists throughout his work. I have quoted 'The Harvest Bow' already in evidence; it occurs too in the totally solemn context of 'Casualty' from the same volume, *Field Work*:

> But my tentative art
> His turned back watches *too*:
> He was blown to bits
> Out drinking in a *curfew* . . .

> Everybody *held*
> His breath and *trembled.*
>   (*FW* 22; emphasis added)

The defamiliarising effect of these lines is highly effective, and the deracinated rhyming is essential to it, but this effectiveness is precisely because, like the bomb in the poem, it is exceptional rather than the rule.

It is instructive to look at some of the metrical misreadings. Mathias tries in this passage to be charitable, as he sees it, about Heaney's metrical failings:

> One becomes aware too of the kinds of rhymes which though in no sense outrageous, are sufficiently unusual to obviate the smallest feeling of rhythmic dullness and predictability. *Cattle/ wall, then/bargain, still/chronicle, stick/attic* – these help to maintain wayward, stumbling movements in the poem, a movement entirely in keeping with cautious farmers and hesitant cattle. (Curtis 21)

Mathias is clearly doing his best, rationalising the roughness as the language appropriate to farmers and cattle (his distinction be-tween the two sounds rather a slender one), and pleading that these barbarous rhymes are 'in no sense outrageous'. All the rhymes he quotes are deliberate employments of the Irish *deibidhe*; Mathias is a good reader of poetry, and his discussion of the consonantal prominence in Heaney's early work is enlighten-ing and informed. So his well-intentioned but uncomprehending reaction to these foreign rhymes might be a further indication that the device is not a safe one to use in an English lyric.

But pragmatism is by no means Heaney's principal motivating concern. His professed anxiety to 'say what happened', in Lowell's terms, makes it undesirable to adopt a poetic form that will draw attention to itself, away from the content of what is being said. This declared ambition – to write naturally – is at least as old as Dante's claim in his exchange with Bonagiunta da Lucca in *Purgatorio* XXIV,[37] quoted in Chapter 5 below. In English, of course, it is familiar from Pope and Wordsworth, as 'what ... was ... ne'er so well expressed' and the language of 'a man speaking to men'.

This 'naturalism' figure is very well attested in Heaney from early on. But its most familiar statement comes in 'Song' from *Field Work* in a line used by Helen Vendler as the title of her book on contemporary poetry:[38]

> And that moment when the bird sings very close
> To the music of what happens.
>
> (*FW* 56)

The reference is to a wonderful moment in the Fenian legends when Finn is asked: 'What music do you like most?' and replies: 'The music of what happens'. It receives several memorable formulations in Heaney's work, such as the often-quoted end of 'North':

> 'Keep your eye clear
> as the bleb of the icicle,
> trust the feel of what nubbed treasure
> your hands have known.'

It is an ambition which requires a transparent linguistic medium. As Hart says: 'Language being what it is, his poems could never attain such perfect objectivity' (77); but the employment of an unfamiliar form that drew attention to itself would be at the opposite extreme. In Chapter 3 below, in considering *Station Island*, I note some striking instances of Heaney's declared view that objects and events generate linguistic form, without conscious human intervention, in keeping with Dryden's Augustan ideal in the Preface to *Religio Laici*.[39]

Not that Heaney's career began like this. The medium of his early poetry, especially the uncollected poems that preceded *Death of a Naturalist*, is extraordinarily dense, and almost solid in its worked materiality. Smith contrasts 'the thickening . . . into the opacities of his earlier work' with a later lexical clarity.[40] Again, because it has been seriously misjudged, it is important to understand that the harshness of diction in this materialist aesthetic was entirely deliberate, although it is a point that might be taken as read in a poet as aware as Heaney is of the lexical harshness of late Yeats. The following judgement in Blake Morrison's book is not untypical of this misunderstanding of the language of *Death of a Naturalist* and *Door into the Dark*:

> Throughout these first two books Heaney looks distinctly
> unhappy in his use of iambic pentameters and quatrains,
> repeatedly wrenching his rhythms and rhymes. To compare his
> work with the work it borrows from is a damaging exercise.
> (Morrison 19)

This is a damaging misinterpretation of a poet who often seemed, in his early work, to be in danger of falling into a metrical overfacility that borders on doggerel. For example, I think there is some truth in Philip Hobsbaum's sophisticated metrical criticisms in his essay 'Craft and Technique in *Wintering Out*': that Heaney had a tendency to adopt 'a rhetorical manner along with a rhythm', and that his attempts to emulate 'the loose quatrain of Patrick Kavanagh' (Curtis 40) tend to fall into patterns which are foreign to it, perhaps because of Heaney's overvirtuoso metrics. Sometimes his ear was – and is – too good for his own good. It is striking that Morrison himself corrects his misinterpretation two sentences later, in noting the tendency in the early work 'to *weigh* inarticulacy against articulation' (I have emphasised 'weigh' to show Morrison's – I think accurate – recognition that this antithetical method is calculated). As Morrison knows, Heaney finds inspiration and devices through 'raids' upon 'the inarticulate' (*P* 47). The result is that the loose and inarticulate occurs side by side with the more obviously 'finished' in the poetry.

The misreading is odd, too, given the venerability of this kind of modernist venture, beginning with Pound's 'goddam iamb' and his claim 'to break the pentameter, that was/ the first heave.'[41] But as Hart puts it: 'The literalists still chastise Heaney (just as they chastised Pound) for recasting the complex patterns of meter, rhyme, assonance, and alliteration of the Gaelic original into a simulacrum of his trademark style' (Hart 154–5). In fact Heaney was never tempted by the modernist attack on the iamb and the pentameter. But his own reminder that he was going 'out of his normal cognitive bounds ... [to] raid the inarticulate' (*P* 47) should have led readers to expect variations from normal practices, including standard metrics.

Whether or not Heaney's variations on the pentameter and the quatrain were always salutary, the deliberateness of the strategy is evident from a consideration of his relation to Kavanagh, who is his principal stylistic influence, at least in the first book. (The materiality of Hughes's language is an influence, too; but there is nothing in him that corresponds to Heaney's vernacular.) A comparison with Kavanagh is an exercise which is enlightening in itself, but also demonstrates the inappropriateness of Morrison's 'damaging exercise'. In his essay 'The Sense of Place' in *Preoccupations*, Heaney considers Kavanagh's opening line: 'The bicycles go by in twos and threes',[42] from 'Inniskeen Road: July Evening', and observes:

> They do not 'pass by' or 'go past' as they would in a more standard English voice or place, and in that little touch Kavanagh touches what I am circling. (*P* 138)

This is a very refined distinction, but Heaney insists that Kavanagh's effect is deliberate by calling it a 'touch', as by a painter. And in *Death of a Naturalist* we can witness similar touches: the most obvious, perhaps, is the last line of the first poem, 'Digging':

> Between my finger and my thumb
> The squat pen rests.
> I'll dig with it.
>
> (*DN* 13)

Since the title of the poem is 'Digging', and that word has occurred twice in the course of it, the word 'dig' cannot take the stress in that last line. In fact the stress must logically be taken by the 'it' – a word which, I think, can take stress *only* in a Northern Irish accent. Moreover, the stressing of 'it' requires a metre which tolerates more prominence in syllables which are normally unstressed than the iambic does: one of the borrowed characteristics of Irish syllabic verse noted by MacDonagh. I take it as obvious that when Heaney later calls 'Digging' 'a big, coarse-grained navvy of a poem' (*P* 43) he is more concerned to describe its language than to criticise it adversely. There were several earlier poems which had more marked stylistic weaknesses and derivativeness which were accordingly omitted from the published volumes; 'Digging' has survived at the head of both volumes of *Selected Poems*.

Kavanagh's influence on Heaney's language is sustained throughout his career, though later on as only one element in a much more diverse technique. A very obvious example of a clear piece of Kavanagh vernacular is the strangely magnificent question 'Who owns them hungry hills?' from 'Shancoduff',[43] mirrored by Heaney's use of the non-standard demonstrative in one of the *Haw Lantern* elegies: 'You/Know all them things' (*HL* 28). This is a clearer case than the bicycles 'going by', about whose non-standard status I am not entirely certain; in fact Smith, in the same essay, makes a good deal of Heaney's prepositions, starting from this passage,[44] following up Heaney's characterisation of them as the 'capillary root' leading down to the essence of place (*P* 138). 'Them' for 'those' is a very obvious non-standard construction to use; but the common factor between the two poets is the use of non-standard forms at all (they have remained curiously absent from mainstream poetry, despite Keats's 'Cockney School' usages).

The pluralism of Heaney's language in *Death of a Naturalist* needs to be stressed as a counter to other misgivings about it, apart from Morrison's. To take a different kind of linguistic reservation: Neil Corcoran criticises another effect in 'Digging', accusing it (again following the poet's lead) of 'theatricality':

> in the false note of the backslapping exclamation. 'By God, the old man could handle a spade', which may register genuine filial pride but which, in a poem rather than a conversation, sounds as if it is trying too hard: what should be all casual ease in fact sounds quite uneasy. (Corcoran 52)

What this fails to allow for, I suggest, is the studied inconsistency of vernacular in this volume, which recurs in a more marked form in the later poetry from *The Haw Lantern* onwards. We might bear in mind Hart's felicitous summary (applied to *Wintering Out*): 'From the phonetic and lexical features of individual words he creates moving dramas' (Hart 49); I think Corcoran is underrepresenting the dramatising of the domestic situation in 'Digging'. As the distracting features of metre become less common, the colloquial usages become more so. The fact that they too do not occur in 'normal' poetic diction does not matter, because their colloquial status, which is the reason for their use, is obvious. Their dramatised vernacular function must not be mistaken for ineptitude.

43

As a final instance of this instability, the Kavanagh-derived vernacular might be contrasted with the use of an excessively magniloquent literary language, employed to ironic effect in 'An Advancement of Learning'. Morrison rightly notes the 'diametrically opposed languages' (Morrison 27) used in the volume, and is alarmed by the register of such a phrase as 'my hitherto snubbed rodent' to describe a rat from which the boy in the poem has first recoiled. This is surely another instance of what Samuel Johnson calls 'harshness of diction', expressing here an awkwardness with the process of 'advancement of learning'. It clearly relates to the dilemma of the writer who is crossing parochial vernacular of Kavanagh's type with more standard diction.

Heaney's interest in this is further evident in what he says about Kavanagh's poem 'Kerr's Ass', which he felicitously describes as a 'risky but successful poem' (P 141). It is the same idea which he characterises elsewhere – even more felicitously – with the word 'chancy', common in Irish usage. The aesthetic of riskiness was established in Christopher Ricks's *Keats and Embarrassment*: the idea that – especially in lyric poetry, with its concentration on the poet's voice – a particular tension can be achieved by manipulation of poetic language in unpredictable ways. Heaney earns our trust that his harshness of diction is deliberate by the extraordinary naturalness he can display in the same volume – for example, in 'bluebottles/ Wove a strong gauze of sound around the smell'. This 'Midas touch' with imagery has been well characterised by John Wilson Foster as 'the axiomatic rightness of the images'.[45] This 'rightness' is one of Heaney's most commonly recognised strengths, and he is able to achieve a mixed style by collocating it with a calculated awkwardness. These two modes – the awkward and the sure – are present together in the celebrated last lines of the book:

> To stare big-eyed Narcissus, into some spring
> Is beneath all adult dignity. I rhyme
> To see myself, to set the darkness echoing.
>
> (*DN* 57)

'Beneath all adult dignity' is the school-English-lesson type of cliché known as 'command of English', as was 'my hitherto snubbed rodent'; here it is tellingly collocated with the brilliantly precise image in the following line.

This dicing with embarrassment is even more overt in some other places in *Death of a Naturalist*, perhaps most prominently in the child-language of the title-poem, which very effectively sets the reader's teeth on edge:

> Miss Walls would tell us how
> The daddy frog was called a bullfrog
> And how he croaked and how the mammy frog
> Laid hundreds of little eggs and this was
> Frogspawn.
>
> (*DN* 15)

In this *rite de passage* poem, the childish language (which is returned to in 'Alphabets' in *The Haw Lantern*, for a different purpose) is effectively counterpointed with the threatening diction of the poem's end, where the adult frogs 'sat/ Poised like mud grenades . . . gathered there for vengeance'. In a longer perspective, such weighted language of innocence is itself poised to explode in an adult world of violence and hardness.

But where does this dicing with embarrassment come from, and what is Heaney's intention in using it? Its origin seems to me surprising but clear. It has played a central part in the poetics of English verse since the fifteenth century and the arguments about 'aureate diction'. The most extreme practitioner of this virtuoso form is Dunbar, who oscillates effortlessly between English, Scots and Latinate English. The occurrence of a 'mixed style' becomes almost a cliché in the sixteenth century, when the emergence of an enriched language (enriched by the proliferation of 'inkhorn terms' through the Renaissance 'Advancement of Learning') led to a double structure on which poets from Donne onwards (and prose-writers too) capitalised with great enthusiasm. Perhaps Dryden marks the point at which the ideal of Augustan clarity banished the enriched register as a respectable element in English style, depriving the language of an effective level of stylistic amplification as practised by prose-writers such as Sir Thomas Browne. Since the eighteenth century, elevated register has always been a marked form, usually ironic and occurring most commonly in the novel. Something of that irony is its effect in this Heaney poem.

There is nothing corresponding to this mixed register in the classical stages of the Irish poetic tradition, when the exigencies of metrical form made consistency difficult enough to achieve without attempting variations on it. In the popular tradition of nineteenth-century songs, a macaronic stream of Irish-English lyrics starts to appear (for example, in the folksong which begins 'One Day for Recreation, *gan éinne beo im chuideactan*'). But nowhere is there any sign of stylistic variation of register in Irish. Before 1700 it was a central – almost *the* essential – property of post-medieval English style; perhaps inevitably, given the increasing lexical hybridisation of the English language. Irish never had sufficiently developed international cultural relations to provide a mixed language. What there is in Irish English, of course, is a macaronic language, made up of Irish and English words. Heaney discusses this acutely in 'Among Schoolchildren': the strangeness of a dialect which contains both the Irish-derived *lachtar* (for a clutch of chickens) and the Latinate 'incubator' (to breed the clutch of chickens) as part of its everyday usage. The problem for the poet of the English lyric about drawing on this register is that it cannot presume intelligibility. It will connote a learnedness which in origin it does not have. (This too, like the *deibidhe*, is exploited more cavalierly by Paul Muldoon than by Heaney: in this line from 'Twice', for instance: 'when I squinnied through it I saw "Lefty", Clery' ['*An Ciotach*'][46] using *ciotach* (in the Muldoon sonnet rhymed with 'Kodak's') for left-handed, an Irish word which occurs in most Irish dialects of English – but not normally in the *TLS*.)

If, then, there was uncertainty about the interpretation of some of the language in Heaney's early poems, there was general agreement about the salient virtues of *Death of a Naturalist*. It was representatively put by Richard Kell in his *Guardian* review: 'what delights, in poem after poem, is the accuracy and freshness with which sense-impressions are recorded': Foster's 'axiomatic rightness'. Terence Brown argues convincingly in his 1975 essay[47] that the ostensible fidelity to fact is always seen from an outside vantage point, giving an impression of solid objectivity. At this stage of Heaney's writing there is no claim to transparency in language; to gain an impression of the material solidarity of the outside world is the poetry's business.

The principal recurrent themes in *Death of a Naturalist*, as they bear on language, have frequently been noted. There is, first, a primitivism of subject, reflected in a primitivism of language. In 'Digging', for example, there is the 'coarse-grained' observation of manual labour, matched by the syntactic crudity of the verbless sentences, the child-language already noted and the awkward stress of the last line. Second, writing is already a conscious theme: the squat pen is already poised to dig metaphorically in 'Digging'. Third, there is a striking recurrence of a contrast between hard and soft materials and surfaces which the language used reflects (even in 'Digging' the spade rasps into gravelly ground and the dug potatoes have a 'cool hardness', in contrast with 'the squelch and slap/ Of soggy peat'). This type of contrast has obvious phonological application; by the time of *Field Work* (1979) Irish speech is described as 'soft-mouthed' in 'The Guttural Muse' (*FW* 28), and a contrast between hard, consonantal English and soft, vocalic Irish has been well established. (The application of this contrast is considered at greater length in the next chapter.) These themes receive varying degrees of prominence throughout Heaney's career, depending on which of a series of topics is being concentrated on. What in retrospect seems most remarkable, and most to justify the enthusiasm with which *Death of a Naturalist* was received (something which might be surprising if some of Morrison's metrical criticisms were generally felt), is the way in which this 'innocent' collection uses a wide range of linguistic registers to achieve a surprising confidence in judgement.

It is evident, then, that the metrical roughness and embarrassing registers of parts of the early poetry are not evidence of a technical limitation that Heaney subsequently grew out of. The evidence is the competent regularity in metre and diction which is normal in Heaney, providing a yardstick against which deviations can be measured and identified as such.

There is another way of seeing Heaney's development after the 1960s which is suggested by Edna Longley's acute, if underdeveloped, observation about *North* which I quoted in the Introduction: 'the gap has narrowed between Heaney's creative and critical idioms' (Curtis 86). I think this is true; but it is not something that has developed between earlier (and, in Longley's view, imaginatively better) Heaney and *North*. It has always been characteristic of him to commentate, implicitly (as in the early poetry) or explicitly (as is increasingly the case in the later poetry), on his own writing. As I claim in Chapter 5 below, he is inclined to be the Dantesque *chiosatore* – glossator – on his own work. It has become fashionable in Chaucer criticism to say that 'the scribes were Chaucer's first critics'; in this sense, Heaney is his own first critic.

In an attempt to clarify this point, I want briefly to use Jakobson's formal categories to describe more exactly Longley's 'creative and critical idioms'. It is true that most of the time we can broadly distinguish creative from critical writing, for practical purposes; but it is much harder to say of particular '*idioms*' (Longley's term) which of the two it belongs to: Eliot's Mallarmé-derived 'to purify the language of the tribe',[48] for example, is the use in a poem of what sounds like a critical programme. Is there anything about the 'idiom' used there which makes it belong to poetry or criticism?

Jakobson's formalist methodology was developed to address exactly this kind of categorical issue: the placing of imaginative, 'literary' language within language as a whole.[49] Of the six constituent elements which Jakobson says are essential in any verbal act (addresser, addressee, context, message, code and contact), three kinds of language have to be distinguished in linguistic use: the everyday, the literary and the critical. These three, corresponding respectively to the context, message and code of the six constituents, are normal language, 'poetic' language, and metalanguage (the critical language used to comment on other kinds of language). To distinguish between them is particularly essential for the interpretation of the writer who feels answerable both to the private and to the public domain, since the latter might be thought to be the particular preserve of 'normal', everyday language.

Heaney's Kavanagh-influenced language presents problems by refusing to sustain this distinction between Jakobson's 'ordinary' language of the everyday, and the 'poetic' language of poetry. This is not merely a terminological opposition. I will argue that throughout his career Heaney expresses doubt about lyric language's capacity to function adequately for what is asked of it. In the terms of the *Crane Bag* interview with Deane, the more desperate the public 'predicament', the more urgent the demand will be for a language 'adequate' to it. In Northern Ireland, increasingly, Heaney represents the public context as imposing more strain on the poetic language than it will bear. As the poetic language falls more evidently short of 'present use', the metalingual, commentating code is invoked more and more. Hence linguistic elements thought proper to critical analysis are invoked increasingly to scrutinise the poetic language, increasingly finding it inadequate.

As a consequence, at several stages of his writing career we find Heaney expressing a craving for adequate poetic language. In the next chapter we find the 'devil-may-careness' with which he constructs the language of the place-name poems in *Wintering Out*. James Joyce is dreamt up at the end of *Station Island* to license Heaney to 'fill the element/ with signatures on your own frequency' (which, as Michael Allen said in reviewing *The Haw Lantern*, he was doing anyway[50]). At the end of the 'South Bank Show' interview with Melvyn Bragg, launching *Seeing Things*, Heaney says that he wants to refuse to be 'obedient to the p's and q's of joined-up prose', so that he can 'write as a poet for a change' (see n. 34 to Introduction). But of course he cannot settle for any of these simplicities; they are not adequate to the predicament.

Next I want to apply these elements of Jakobson's methodology to the questions of metre and diction discussed above. A poetic analysis, whose primary concern is with the verbal message, will give prominence to such matters as whether a writer uses Irish or English metrical forms. Heaney, as I said at the beginning of this chapter, moves from the employment of variable, overnoticeable language ('harsh' diction of various kinds) to an attempt to achieve a more 'natural' language. This involves a shift in prominence from the poetic function to the ordinary or casual, with a corresponding levelling out of diction. It applies equally to metre: it will involve a movement from abnormal metrical effects (the *deibidhe* rhymes, prominent unstressed syllables, and so on) to a more universal employment of the home metre. It was the misleading signals that the 'home key' (the norms of Shakespearian iambic) sent out that led to the uncertainty experienced by Mathias and Morrison; if the norm is traditional English metre and scansion, then the occasional use of particular non-English metrical effects will be problematic. Morrison's 'damaging exercise' of comparing Heaney's early rhyme-schemes and metrics with his apparent source is founded on the misplaced certainty of what the norm here is thought to be.

But of course, Heaney's divided pieties are perfectly represented by this problematic set of correspondences. Finally, I want to review the other prominent aspects, as well as metre, of the language of the first two books in the light of Jakobson's methodology. The first theme I noted in *Death of a Naturalist*, its primitivism, is expressed uncomplicatedly by its language. The verbless sentences, unstable register, awkward stresses and child-language are all self-consciously 'literary' uses of language which define the theme by departure from norms. Writing itself as a theme is more complicated, because it involves directly the creative and critical 'idioms'; that is, writing as its own subject. So already in *Death of a Naturalist*, part of the volume's theme is its own code; repeatedly throughout the volume metalinguistic references focus attention on the code in a way which is typical of the self-conscious language-user (the red blackberries 'inked up' in 'Blackberry-Picking'; the 'clean new music' that gave 'back your own call' in 'Personal Helicon'; the 'definition' of land and sea in 'Lovers on Aran'; Synge on Aran has a 'hard pen scraping in his head', like the poet's brainchild 'pottering' in 'Poem, for Marie'; the folksingers and St Francis are composers). Although it is never again so insistent a theme, the metalinguistic as subject rather than commentary never disappears from Heaney's practice. An obvious recurrence is the 'Scribes' and other 'book' poems in *Station Island*; but it is present to a greater or lesser degree throughout his writing.

But that is looking far ahead. Still in the 1960s, there is a striking change in the language between the characteristic heaviness of *Death of a Naturalist* and the short poems at the beginning of *Door into the Dark*. Seamus Deane, in *A Short History of Irish Literature*, distinguishes between the first two volumes rather cryptically by saying that *Death of a Naturalist* laments lost innocence, while *Door into the Dark* 'finds ways to dramatize' this.[51] The first three short poems are entirely lacking in the 'opacity' of the first book; they also lack its directness, remaining slight, if suggestive. The volume hits its stride with 'The Forge', whose first line provides the volume's title. From this point on, the general tendency is towards greater regularity of form. The metrical and dictional roughnesses are much less evident, and the iambic 'home key' is commoner and often positively metronomic. In two major poems – on the themes respectively of inadequacy in language and the technique [*techne*] of the artisan – the iambic is as regular as it is in Elizabethan sonnets:

> When you have nothing more to say, just drive
> ('The Peninsula', *DD* 21)

> And left them gaping at his Midas touch.
> ('Thatcher', *DD* 20)

It would be simplistic, however, to ignore the language of the book's early poems on the grounds that they are slighter. There is experimentation throughout with regular forms (in sonnets such as 'The Forge', for example), and impressionistic irregularity (like the glancing opening horse-poem 'Night-Piece'). Even within the same group, 'A Lough Neagh Sequence', we find the excessively endstopped regularity of 'Up the Shore': 'The lough will claim a victim every year' (*DD* 38), next to 'Beyond Sargasso', the irregularity of which is reminiscent of the 'Proteus' section of Joyce's *Ulysses*:

> A gland agitating
> mud two hundred miles in-
> land, a scale of water
> on water working up
> estuaries . . .
> (*DD* 39)

What is more, classical Irish or regular/irregular English are not the only metrical forms in contention; the next three poems of 'A Lough Neagh Sequence' develop the *terza rima* which was inchoate in *Death of a Naturalist* in 'The Early Purges' and 'Lovers on Aran', and becomes an important staple form in *Station Island* and *Seeing Things*.

Some generalisation is possible in comparing the language with that of the previous book: it is lighter, and the consonantal thickness accurately noted by Mathias is much less evident. The *deibidhe* rhymes (which are still there: for instance, *rusting/ring* in the brilliantly imagist 'The Forge') are less noticeable; the odd seven-syllable line seems an almost accidental variant on the commoner octosyllabic. In 'The Given Note' there is a new timbre, one which was subsequently developed more by Paul Muldoon than by Heaney himself. The book also has one of Heaney's finest, most Dantesque pieces of 'axiomatic rightness' in imagery, the burnt gorse bush in 'Whinlands':

> Put a match under
> Whins, they go up of a sudden.
> They make no flame in the sun
> But a fierce heat tremor
>   (*DD* 47)

We have here, as often in this book (the 'smoke of flies' in 'At Ardboe Point' is another such example), a sense of an extraordinarily penetrating descriptive talent waiting for its compelling subject.

What has always been seen as the book's most important poem – 'Bogland', with which it ends – is a more significant formal departure. It is the first occurrence of what Morrison and others have suggestively termed the 'artesian stanza' of *North*, here used for archaeological application too. In theme, the primitivism of *Death of a Naturalist* has modulated into a more urbane antiquarianism. Similarly, the violent imagery has been placed in a dream world, by a kind of metonymic transformation, and the putrefaction concentrates on the fruitfulness it promotes, which was only dimly implied in the earlier book. In a development which will have enormous repercussions in the next two volumes, the poems 'Undine', 'Cana Revisited', 'Bann Clay', 'Bogland' and 'A Lough Neagh Sequence' are all concerned with the future products of underground or underwater chemistry.

It seems to me that there were more changes in subject and theme between Heaney's first two books than is often recognised. The change in *North* (or perhaps in parts of *Wintering Out*) towards a more public declaratory poetry – more conscious, that is to say, of context than in the previous poems, with their concentration on the poetic message and its commenting code – has been commonly noted. So has the wish to move (or to return) towards the quotidian with the publication of *Field Work*. But there is also in *Door into the Dark* a move of a different kind, towards a more internalised focus on the poet/addresser. It is a movement which makes the leap towards the dutiful and public in *North* a more marked shift than it would have been from *Death of a Naturalist*. The strange intensity of this introverted but lighter language is especially notable in the early poems in the volume, such as 'Dream' (*DD* 15).

The best discussion of this aspect of *Door into the Dark* (indeed, the best discussion of the book from any viewpoint) is Henry Hart's reading of it as the first stage of a mystical progress which culminates in *Seeing Things*. Hart's chapter 'The Poetry of Meditation' (32–48) shows the book to be radically different in meaning from *Death of a Naturalist*, linking it with the great mystics of the Western tradition: St Ignatius, St Teresa, *The Cloud of Unknowing*, their interpreter Evelyn Underhill, and Thomas Merton. The linguistic implications of this are considerable, particularly for the question of inadequate language which Hart (again anticipating *Seeing Things*) relates to the mystical *via negativa* as the methodical access to certainty of perception. Rather surprisingly in the context of this book, but with a bearing on the conception of language that emerges from 'Alphabets' in *The Haw Lantern* onwards, Hart sees Heaney as celebrating the written rather than the spoken:

> If a logocentric preference for the spoken has devalued the written in Western thought, as Derrida insists, Heaney tends to celebrate the concrete accomplishment of writing over the evanescence of speech. (Hart 38)

Hence landscape is seen as written form waiting to be decoded. (Later I argue against this, in favour of a more standard, binary view of linguistic construction in Heaney; but I think Hart's reading of *Door into the Dark* makes it easier to see the book as a stage on the way to *Wintering Out*.)

But the most important thing Hart does with *Door into the Dark* is to see the concentration of images of femininity, productivity and water in mystical terms, in poems such as 'Rite of Spring', 'Undine' and 'Mother'. In the mystical tradition of affective piety, the link between perception and sexuality has always been crucial. In Dionysian works like *The Cloud of*

Unknowing such images are connected with concentrated explora-
tion of the signifying power of language.

The new set of images to do with water, the feminine and
productivity are also, perhaps, germinated in the second element
of the hard/soft antitheses noted above from 'Digging' onwards,
anticipating the way phonology carries much of the meaning-
power of language in *Wintering Out*. The fecundity of this
imagery represents an incubation of history and ideas which is
used in productive but unsettling ways from this volume to *Station
Island*. But the most important formal development beyond *Death
of a Naturalist* is the pared-down 'artesian stanza' which drives its
way through much of the book's second half. Of this book's
poems, the last and most important one, 'Bogland', employs the
stanza to greatest effect. Equally significantly, it moves towards
the concerns to which that stanza drills down in the following two
volumes:

> They've taken the skeleton
> Of the Great Irish Elk
> Out of the peat, set it up
> An astounding crate full of air.
>
> Butter sunk under
> More than a hundred years
> Was recovered salty and white.
> The ground itself is kind, black butter
>
> Melting and opening underfoot,
> Missing its last definition
> By millions of years.
> They'll never dig coal here,
>
> Only the waterlogged trunks
> Of great firs, soft as pulp.
> Our pioneers keep striking
> Inwards and downwards,
>
> Every layer they strip
> Seems camped on before.
> The bogholes might be Atlantic seepage.
> The wet centre is bottomless.
>
> (*DD* 55–6)

This connects with the images of water and the feminine that have
been developing throughout the book; but more obviously it

points forward to the 'Bog' poems, where those imagistic associations are present too. There are other, lesser connections between *Door into the Dark* and *Wintering Out*: for example, the hymnlike *dinnseanchas* run of place-names in the beautiful poem 'Shoreline', ending:

> Strangford, Arklow, Carrickfergus,
> Belmullet and Ventry
> Stay, forgotten like sentries.
>
> (*DD* 52)

'Bogland' was published in 1969, before Heaney read Glob's *The Bog People*, and it demonstrates the truth of Heaney's saying, of his encounter with that book, 'my roots were crossed with my reading'.[52] The transition from *Door into the Dark* to *Wintering Out* is one of the volume-borders in the *New Selected Poems* which is hardest to spot: from 'Bogland' to 'Bog Oak'. This is surprising, because *Door into the Dark* has generally been thought of as one of Heaney's lesser achievements, while Neil Corcoran's view that *Wintering Out* is 'the seminal single volume of the post-1970 period of English poetry'[53] would command a good deal of assent.

What is certain is that the transition between these books marks Heaney's movement towards a confident poetic which is altogether his own for the first time. No doubt this had much to do with his reading of Glob, which occasioned the writing of 'The Tollund Man'. Heaney called it 'a moment of commitment not in the political sense but in the deeper sense of your life, committing yourself to something. I think that brought me to a new possibility of seriousness in the poetic enterprise'.[54] This commitment replaces the vaguer commitment to an Irish poetic tradition in which Heaney had always been uneasy and unfulfilled. The issues around him were too serious to make the formalities of 'the poetic enterprise' an end in itself without reference to its wider 'present use'. No doubt this is what Heaney saw when he wrote away for Glob's book with such excitement. The language which up to this point, despite Heaney's misgivings about its intelligibility, has often seemed to have a power of expression and analysis beyond what was asked of it has an image of compelling power to work with in order to test its adequacy for the predicament of Northern Ireland after 1969.

Phonetics and Feeling

Wintering Out, North *and* Field Work
(1970s Heaney)

At the end of the last chapter I quoted Neil Corcoran's observation that *Wintering Out* was the 'seminal single volume of the post-1970 period of English poetry'.[1] The staple now is 'normal' language, as used in a locality, in place of the wrestling with the demands of two established poetic languages evident in Heaney's earlier poetry: the post-Irish tradition represented by un-English metres and diction, and the 'home key' of post-Shakespearian English usage. Corcoran sees this reliance on local usage, the 'introducing [of] a lexicon and a register of pronunciation distinct from "received" or Standard English',[2] as signalled in the volume's opening poem's 'postmodernist' redefinition of its Standard English title:

> FODDER
>
> Or, as we said,
> *fother*, I open
> my arms for it
> again.
>   (WO 13)

Corcoran is certainly right to see this as a moment of significance, and for the reasons he gives. We might go on to note – following the concerns of Chapter 1 here – that it is the most overt intervention of the commentary into the text so far. The opening of the poem is a kind of parenthesis, such as is usually found as a textual footnote. We see that the invasion of the imaginative idiom by the critical is therefore a figure for the supplantation of Standard English by local usage. Part I of the book, which is two-thirds of the whole and is generally agreed to be the best part of it, is taken up almost obsessively with local linguistic terms and commentary on them. Obligations to both literary traditions are being abandoned as bad masters, as attention is turned to actual linguistic usage, which is the lifeblood of all literary practice. To quote again from the *Irish Times* interview with Elgy Gillespie: he is turning to 'writing poems . . . that grow out of words and ways of talking'.[3]

The matter of pronunciation raised by the word *fother* is most prominent in three poems that I will soon spend some time on: 'Anahorish', 'Broagh' and 'A New Song'. But there is one other important new development which is central to my subject: the prominent use of the terminology of linguistic analysis in the early part of the book.

'Gifts of Rain', a poem which most critics of Heaney have felt to be significant without quite being able to demonstrate why, is suffused with linguistic reference used metaphorically. From 'he begins to *sense* weather/ by his skin' (23; emphasis added), with its suggestion of interpretation, the poem proceeds through the fording of life by 'Soundings'. After Foster's 'axiomatic rightness' of the image 'like a cut swaying/ its red spoors through a basin' (WO 23), the linguistic metaphor turns to concentrate entirely on the auditory. The 'world-schooled ear' interprets the various noises of water, finally seen in expressly phonological terms:

> The tawny guttural water
> spells itself: Moyola . . .
>
> bedding the locale
> in the utterance,
> reed music, an old chanter
>
> breathing its mists
> through vowels and history.
> (WO 25)

Here the interpretation of naturally produced sound ('reed music') and the linguistically constructed ('utterance') are made semantically inextricable. Obviously, the subject of water as an incubatory element promoting fertility, noted in *Door into the Dark*, has an almost mythological centrality here, as in several of the poems in *Wintering Out*. Other themes, too, are continuous from the earlier volumes: primitivism is now firmly wedded to the artesian stanza. Even 'Anahorish', the 'place of clear water', keeps in touch with its origins by ending with dunghills, linking back to the fertilising water of its opening.

The linguistic metaphors of 'Gifts of Rain' (which I find, despite its imagistic brilliance, lacking in the sense of clear purpose that characterises most of the poems in Part I of *Wintering Out*) occur in various forms in many of the other poems in Part I. In 'Land' the poem's speaker lies listening for Morse-like 'drumming' from the earth (WO 22). The child hiding in the willow tree in 'Oracle' is called 'its listening familiar' (WO 28), as if he were nothing but 'mouth and ear', 'lobe and larynx'. In one of Heaney's most beautiful poems, 'The Backward Look', the snipe's dive is metamorphosed into language:

> A stagger in air
> as if a language
> failed, a sleight
> of wing.
> > (WO 29)

This poem goes on to play with the Irish kennings for snipe, *gabhairín reo*:

> little goat of the air,
> of the evening,
>
> little goat of the frost,

calling the sounds he makes, in a striking series of linguistic metamorphoses, 'dialect', 'variants' and 'transliterations', as his tail-feathers are 'drumming elegies'.

One of the best-known poems of the series is 'Traditions', which begins:

> Our guttural muse
> was bulled long ago

by the alliterative tradition,
her uvula grows

vestigial.

(WO 31)

There is a very learned point lurking here. Heaney was enthusiastic about language classes with John Braidwood and G. B. Adams at Queen's (Morrison 40), particularly enjoying phonetics, and he is applying some specialist competence in this poem. Standard English has no uvular consonants, though several dialects have a uvular /r/ (for example, Geordie: see Tom McArthur's *Oxford Companion to the English Language*, 437.[4] McArthur says, with adventitious aptness for the context in Heaney, that this 'Northumberland burr' is 'widely regarded as a speech defect' [*ibid*]). 'Traditions' is a humorous poem which has been taken much too solemnly; it goes on to list Irish vestigial Elizabethanisms: 'deem', 'allow', as well as the Scottish consonants that shuttle 'obstinately/ between bawn and mossland' (WO 32), and ends with Bloom's alienation in Dublin related to that of MacMorris, the stage Irishman in *Henry V*, at the Globe. Three poems later, 'The Wool Trade' uses as its epigraph the most familiar Joycean statement of this linguistic imperialism, Stephen Dedalus's bitter reflection about the English Dean of Studies in *A Portrait of the Artist as a Young Man*: 'How different are the words *home, Christ, ale, master*, on his lips and on mine.'[5]

The centrality of language as subject as well as medium is indisputable from the outset in *Wintering Out*. The aspiration towards Irish metrical forms is much less in evidence; it occurs occasionally, much in the way that alliteration was a lightly carried item in the repertoire of a Victorian poet: there is a striking *deibidhe* rhyme in 'A New Song' which significantly rhymes the English dialectal land-term 'bawn' with the Irish dialectal archaeological 'bullaun'. But piety towards another venerable Irish tradition is now much more prominent. The old Irish form *dinnseanchas*, poetry of locality, with its rootedness in Irish place-names, is a much more promising formality for a poet of Heaney's lyric inclinations than the uncertain assonating of Larminie. But it covers much of the same ground in its concentration on the terminology of linguistics, especially phonology. And it is in the place-name poems in *Wintering Out* that the centrality of sound analysis in the poems I have just considered is most programmatic.

As the quotation from the Gillespie interview shows, Heaney clearly sees the fidelity to place in these poems as a solution to a problem of affiliation. After the unduly material feel of the poems in *Death of a Naturalist*, he now makes for the first time a claim that becomes increasingly insistent in his commentary: the claim that the poem is somehow writing itself, without the poet's mediation: poems 'that *grow out* of words and ways of talking'. This is one way of saying that the poems simply dramatise the language of place that speaks for itself, in the *dinnseanchas* tradition.

By employing *dinnseanchas* Heaney is serving several purposes. I mentioned in Section 3 of the Introduction his discussion in 'The Sense of Place' of Montague's 'learned landscape', especially in the epoch-making volume *The Rough Field*, published in the same year as *Wintering Out* (1972). *Rough Field* translates the Irish *Garbh Faiche*, in English 'Garvaghey', where Montague comes from. (As a matter of interest, 'Garvaghey' occurs (as 'Garvaghy') in P. W. Joyce's *Irish Local Names Explained*;[6] neither 'Broagh' nor 'Anahorish' – both small townlands – is included.) In 'The Sense of Place', in *Preoccupations*, Heaney shows how Montague's etymologising of the place-name contrasts with Kavanagh's more innocent reaction to place, in poems such as 'Shancoduff' (a place-name which, as it happens, would lend itself very suitably to such analysis as something like 'dark antiquity'). This attitude to place is paralleled later by Brian Friel's play *Translations*,[7] which seeks similarly to find the meaning of a place in the surface structure of its naming, through etymological analysis. *Wintering Out* marks Heaney's transition from an impressionistic poet of place like Kavanagh to a symbolist, analytical one more like Montague.

There is still, of course, an 'innocent', unanalysed enthusiasm for naming. In the occasional regular metrical forms we can hear more than previously the prosody of Yeats. The beginning of 'A New Song', 'I met a girl from Derrygarve', has an affinity with such evocative Yeatsian openings as 'The light of evening, Lissadell'.[8] But there is no doubt that the matter of primary linguistic importance is the new concern with etymology. The 'gradients of consonant' and 'vowel-meadows' are first mentioned in 'Anahorish' (*WO* 16), where as yet they read somewhat cryptically. Their employment there is evocative, but lacks the toponymic definition that comes to give them meaning. Neither is there any doubt about the liberating effect of the etymological delving on Heaney's imagination. Of the etymological poems, he says in the Deane *Crane Bag* interview:

> I had a great sense of release as they were being written, a joy and devil-may-careness, and that convinced me that one could be faithful to the nature of the English language – for in some senses these poems are erotic mouth-music by and out of the Anglo-Saxon tongue – and, at the same time, be faithful to one's own non-English origin – for me that is County Derry.[9]

What is striking here is the fact that it seeks simultaneous connection with and detachment from both the English and Irish traditions. Again, it is notable that the language – 'the tongue' – is English, and it is the 'origins' (we should recall the 'politics and anthropology of our condition' in the same interview) which are Irish.

We might note in passing that this wish to be simultaneously faithful to the local Irish origin in County Derry and to 'the nature of the English language' has a well-established heritage in Irish writing in English. One of the most interesting things in David Lloyd's essay is his quoting of Denis Florence McCarthy's introduction to *The Book of Irish Ballads* in 1846, an important document of the Young Irelanders' nationalist programme. McCarthy proposes that a distinctive identity for Irish literature in English might be founded on a knowledge of the ballad poetry. Lloyd quotes his enthusiastic objective:

> That we can be thoroughly Irish in our writings without ceasing to be English; that we can be faithful to the land of our birth without being unfaithful to that literature which has been 'the nursing mother of our minds' . . .[10]

Lloyd is surely right to hear an echo of this programme in Heaney's sense of double inheritance in his comments about the language of *Wintering Out*.

The sense of mouth-music release is very evident (too much so, perhaps) in a poem like 'Toome', with its 'soft blastings/ *Toome,*

Toome', and in the 'vowelling embrace' in 'A New Song'. In another important essay on language and sentiment in *Preoccupations*, 'Feeling into Words', Heaney cites W.R. Rodgers (a poet, like Hopkins, 'much lured by alliteration': *P* 44) for the contrast between Ulster 'spiky consonants' and 'the round fit of the gab in southern' Irish mouths (*P* 44–5). Rodgers's wonderful Ulster consontantal line, quoted by Heaney, is: 'tin-cans, fricatives, fornication, staccato talk'. 'Toome' and the 'vowelling embrace' are Heaney's light-hearted, 'sissy' vocalic rejoinders to the favourers of harsh consonants who 'find the soft ones sissy' in Rodgers's poem, where the vowel–consonant structure, which in 'Anahorish' was used only descriptively, is made an Irish–English opposition for the first time, as it is repeatedly thereafter.

It might be noted, too, that the rhythm of 'A New Song' sounds more like Tennyson's 'Brook' than Austin Clarke:

> But now our river tongues must rise
> From licking deep in native haunts
> To flood, with vowelling embrace
> Demesnes staked out in consonants.
>
> (WO 33)

Part of the release that Heaney described to Deane has to do with feeling free to write in the traditional 'lyrical' English vein for which his good ear equips him naturally (and which Hobsbaum, often constructively, inhibited). But it should also be noted that this Tennysonian iambic is let down with a bump by the poem's *deibidhe* ending: 'A vocable, as rath and bullaun' (WO 33). The integrity of the dialect usages is maintained by not highlighting the last two nouns here with italics or quotation marks; they are a part of the text, forceful as their intrusion into the metre is.

It has always been recognised that the most important of these poems is 'Broagh', in which Heaney's interest and competence in linguistics are used with considerable cunning, as they were in 'Fodder'. 'Broagh' is so dense with what can only be called – again in Jakobson's terms – distinctive features (that is, meanings established by linguistic oppositions) that it has to be quoted in full:

> Riverbank, the long rigs
> ending in broad docken

and a canopied pad
down to the ford.

The garden mould
bruised easily, the shower
gathering in your heelmark
was the black O

in *Broagh*,
its low tattoo
among the windy boortrees
and rhubarb-blades

ended almost
suddenly, like that last
gh the strangers found
difficult to manage.
(WO 27)

This poem has attracted a great deal of attention – most importantly, of course, from Heaney himself in his 1983 John Malone Memorial Lecture 'Among Schoolchildren', and more recently from Tom Paulin in an Open University broadcast, reprinted in *The English Review*.[11] Paulin's acute analysis draws attention to the mixture of dialect features in the poem: the dialectal vocabulary is striking, drawn from Irish [*boortrees* – elder], Scots [*rigs*] and English [*docken*] usage: the full Northern Irish linguistic complex.

The most significant feature is the three uses of italics in the passage which, in effect, mark off the three terms as phonemes: that is, notional phonic entities that cannot be enunciated. This is clearest in the '*gh* the strangers found/ difficult to manage'. This Derry-speaker's shibboleth *is* difficult to manage because it is not clear how the voice, as distinct from the eye, is meant to realise it. Is it a gesture at the phoneme /x/ itself (in which case it is literally unpronounceable, being only a contrastive item in the language system), or is the reader – often a 'stranger' – meant to attempt to pronounce it?

One of the most stimulating – albeit limited – early discussions of Heaney's language was John Wilson Foster's 'The Poetry of Seamus Heaney', written in 1974, between *Wintering Out* and *North*.[12] Having dealt in an almost comic way with the association between darkness and Catholicism in *Door into the Dark* –

the hunters in 'Bait' act 'under cover of darkness as befits dastardliness' (40) – Foster proceeds to the 'topographical poems' in which, he says acutely, 'parts of speech and parts of language are identified' (43). What is more interesting in the essay, though, is what he says about the *gh* of 'Broagh'. Foster says that Heaney erroneously implies that the velar fricative *gh* (the phoneme /x/) was 'a native Irish rather than an English sound'. But Heaney's point is precisely that for the native Irish sound (as at the end of 'Lough'), familiar locally 'to Protestant and Catholic alike', the Old English spelling system can offer only an approximation from within the resources of its own orthography. This is the now-obsolete Germanic velar fricative, as in Chaucer's 'knight' [/knixt/], which of course has no historic relation to the sound at the end of the Celtic word *bruach*, 'riverbank'. The supplying of this non-native orthographic form is no help with the re-creation of the pronunciation to which spelling, in its clumsy way, aspires. (It is, of course, a fundamental axiom in phonology that the speaker of one phonological system is initially trapped in it, and will supply features of it as the nearest approximations to unfamiliar sounds in another language.)

Heaney is making the same point as he was in 'Fodder'/*fother*. It is an identical irony, because in both cases the spelling symbol drafted in to supply the deficiency is in fact a native English phoneme (in 'Fodder' the voiced /th/) which cannot solve the problem. It is a perfect symbol of difference, as also are the lexical elements in 'Broagh', where the effect is a half-comic exclusiveness (one confirmed, perhaps, by the odd term 'the strangers', which is mischievously reminiscent of the Irish-American sentimental song 'Galway Bay': 'Oh the strangers came and tried to teach us their ways'). Like Tony Harrison (though less noticeably), the parochial poet here is cunningly 'occupy[ing]/ your lousy leasehold Poetry',[13] both by planting in it sounds that are difficult to reproduce, and by taking over words of English origin but now of local Irish provenance.

There is a final, even more significant point about 'Broagh' which is generally, true of the pluralist language of the 'place-naming', poems in Part I of *Wintering Out*. I have been emphasising throughout that Heaney's work is never to be taken in isolation from its social context. It is obvious that the tendency of this multistranded language (English, Scottish and Irish) is to create an inextricable whole. Heaney spells this out in the Gillespie *Irish Times* interview: the strangers who are outsiders to South Derry can't manage that *gh*; 'but Protestant and Catholic can say it perfectly in this part of the world' (see n. 3 above).

This is a much more effective takeover of poetry than the attempt to smuggle in metrical effects. As a device, it is also very versatile, not confined to such phonological niceties as those considered here. Localities have their distinctive syntax too: 'The Last Mummer', for example, dialectally 'catches the stick in his fist' (WO 18).

Heaney's first great statement poem, and the one that made it impossible not to see him as a writer of the first significance thereafter (as he senses in the passage quoted at the end of Chapter 1[14]), is 'The Tollund Man', which is a kind of metamorphic *dinnseanchas* poem:

> Something of his sad freedom
> As he rode the tumbril
> Should come to me, driving,
> Saying the names
>
> Tollund, Grauballe, Nebelgard,
> Watching the pointing hands
> Of country people,
> Not knowing their tongue.
>
> Out there in Jutland
> In the old man-killing parishes
> I will feel lost,
> Unhappy and at home.
> (WO 48)

The connection here with Northern Ireland is primarily contextual, but it is also formal. This is an Irish poem, full of echoes. The Northern Irish parallel of 'four young brothers, trailed/ For miles along the lines' brings to mind Yeats's 'The Stare's Nest by my Window' from 'Meditations in Time of Civil War':

> Last night they trundled down the road
> That dead young soldier in his blood.[15]

Furthermore, it is a recognisable Heaney poem: when the executed victim was exhumed from the Danish bog, they found 'His last gruel of winter seeds/ Caked in his stomach' (*WO* 47), which cannot fail to evoke 'Requiem for the Croppies':

> The pockets of our great coats full of barley ...
> The hillside blushed, soaked in our broken wave ...
> And in August the barley grew up out of the grave.
> (*DD* 24)

Heaney discusses the two poems together, along with Yeats's war poetry, in 'Feeling into Words' (*P* 56–9). The most important thing about 'The Tollund Man' is that it serves notice, more signally than any other poem in *Wintering Out*, that Heaney is now embarking on the painful process of writing his 'Meditations in Time of Civil War', the 'responsible *tristia*' of the 'inner émigré', Ovid or Mandelstam.

This is an exacting programme which will not tolerate much deflection or temporising. It means that another important Gaelic-derived tradition, in evidence for the first time in *Wintering Out*, does not survive long in Heaney's practice. It is one which, like the metrical devices, Heaney does not use as a primary element in his poetry, though other Northern Irish poets do (again, Muldoon is the principal case). Thomas MacDonagh quotes Kuno Meyer as saying of the old Gaelic poets: 'the half-said thing to them is dearest'.[16] A tendency towards the cryptic, the elliptical and the half-stated is evident in Muldoon, in tendencies in him that have been characterised as postmodern; in the best traditions of postmodernism, the roots of part of the collage can be found in an area which is far from modern.

A number of poems in *Wintering Out* show this inclination. Both 'Serenades' and 'Somnambulist' might well be attributed to Muldoon if they occurred in a quotation competition (as might the later 'Widgeon', which is dedicated to Muldoon – if it were not so well known):

> The Irish nightingale
> Is a sedge-warbler
> A little bird with a big voice
> Kicking up a racket all night.
>
> Not what you'd expect
> From the musical nation.
> I haven't even heard one.
> (*WO* 62)

To complain of the noise made by a bird you have never heard is decidedly Muldonian. So is the cryptic delicacy of the imagist 'Somnambulist':

> Nestrobber's hands
> and a face in its net of gossamer;
>
> he came back weeping
> to unstarch the pillow
>
> and freckle her sheets
> with tiny yolk.
>
> (WO 63)

In particular this poem is redolent of Muldoon's brilliant and painful 'Aisling' from *Quoof*.[17]

It may seem odd to dwell at some length on a procedure that was short-lived in Heaney's poetry. It belongs with the etymologising of 'Broagh' and 'Toome', which Heaney found a release but came largely to abandon as an indulgence. These 'half-said' things serve the same poetic purpose as the calculated use of rough diction and metre in *Death of a Naturalist* by establishing this poetry and subject as separate from the main tradition. But if they were short-lived in the poetry, they became absolutely crucial – perhaps the staple recourse – to Heaney's criticism, as has frequently been recognised (most recently in Stan Smith's interesting, if choppy, essay in *The Chosen Ground*, 1992[18]). The postmodernist play with etymologies, and with meanings that lurk repressed between the ostensible ones, has become central even to the titles of Heaney's critical books, especially the ambiguities of the name *The Government of the Tongue*. (And of course, it remains prominent in the *titles* of poems and collections of poems: *Seeing Things* is the obvious example.)

But I want to turn now to the emergence of the next volume, *North*, and the relationship between its language and its responsibilities. In its anxiety about public statement, it could not be further from any form of release and self-indulgence, whether etymological or half-said, in austere contrast with both the material opacity of the language of *Death of a Naturalist*, and the devil-may-careness of *Wintering Out*. It will require a return to the stress on the production of a transparent medium for its expression. There is some clear continuity from *Wintering Out*;

most obviously, 'The Tollund Man' is the first of the 'Bog' poems which are the centre of *North*. But the next book's method of accommodating its poetic to its public meaning is a very different departure for Heaney.

North: 'clear/ as the bleb of the icicle'

If the early reactions to *Wintering Out* were uncertain, albeit enthusiastic, all the reviews of *North* displayed considerable certainty, though it was by no means all on the same side of the question, or about the same things. But most of them noted the transparent medium to which Heaney has been aspiring since poems such as 'Oracle' in *Wintering Out*, and which he has gone on expressing as an ideal up to the image of crystalline water at the end of the title-poem of *Seeing Things*. This aspiration is stated more eloquently than ever before at the end of the title-poem, in the collective Northern wisdom of the advice attributed to 'the longship's swimming tongue':

> 'Keep your eye clear
> as the bleb of the icicle,
> trust the feel of what nubbed treasure
> your hands have known.'
>
> (N 20)

This adjuration to clarity and transparency is the same advice that the poet will receive from Joyce in *Station Island*, and it is the literary inference he will draw from various non-Northern sources. Several of the early reviewers of *North* took the poet at his word. Conor Cruise O'Brien, in *The Listener*, paid tribute to the achieved transparency:

> I had the uncanny feeling, reading these poems, *of listening to the thing itself*, the actual substance of historical agony and dissolution, the tragedy of a people in a place: the Catholics of Northern Ireland.[19]

Morrison takes the same view: 'at several points in *North* one feels that Heaney is not writing his poems but having them written for him, his frieze composed almost in spite of him by the "anonymities" of race and religion' (Morrison 68).

Already there is in Morrison some suggestion of unease at the abdication of responsibility in the wish to write through a transparent medium. In Heaney's later poetry – especially in *Station Island*, as I argue in Chapter 3 below – the attempt to show 'the music of what happens' playing itself without the intermediacy of the musician/poet will be an important part of the treatment of the poetic voice. This distancing of utterance, or abdication of responsibility for it, is an important development in *North*, as the clarity of 'the bleb of the icicle' is aimed at. In the title-poem, the unlikely verbaliser is the 'longship's swimming tongue' which instructs the poet to 'lie down in the word-hoard' and 'compose in darkness'. This attempt to let the event or object do its own talking and judging by this kind of far-fetched prosopopoeia comes to a head in the crypticism of parts of *Station Island*, where (as described in the next chapter) the voice that urges dialect adeptness on the poet comes 'out of the field across the road'.

Morrison's unease with the way the violence of *North* is allowed to speak for itself had been put with far greater force by Ciaran Carson in his fiercely hostile review of the book in the *Honest Ulsterman*, where he refers to the poet as 'the laureate of violence – a mythmaker, an anthropologist of ritual killing . . . the world of megalithic doorways and charming, noble barbarity'.[20] Carson famously concludes: 'Everyone was anxious that *North* should be a great book; when it turned out it wasn't, it was treated as one anyway, and made into an Ulster '75 Exhibition of the Good that can come out of Troubled Times.' Behind this last phrase, and also maybe behind some of Heaney's anxieties in the volume, can be heard an echo of the disturbing Brechtian *mot*: 'There is an old Chinese curse, "May you be born in interesting times". But for the poet this is not a curse but a blessing.'

What is most interesting from a critical viewpoint about Carson's attack is its own demonstrable anxiety to be final and incontrovertible. Hence the curiously unexamined absolute term 'a great book': a poet of Carson's sophistication does not need to be reminded that there is no such unequivocal thing. It is the first occurrence of what I called the 'major–minor' debate with reference to David Lloyd's essay on Heaney at the beginning of the Introduction. Carson is showing the same haste as the other reviewers to see what exactly the yield of this drilling process into history and the Northern consciousness has proved to be. Declan Kiberd, in his introduction to the section on 'Contemporary Irish Poetry' in *The Field Day Anthology of Irish Writing*, sounds less certain about this archaeological 'sense of poetry as a dig, and of the poem as something lifted out of a boggy consciousness' (vol. III, 1315). But he does see the venture as serious, if not always productive: 'in only a few poems has even Heaney managed to capture the appalling intensity of that conflict' (*ibid*).

The book's structure certainly has an air of demonstration to it, as Edna Longley pointed out in her discussion of the language of *North* in the review reprinted in Curtis, and in her *Poetry in the Wars*:[21] 'in contrast with the fecund variety of *Wintering Out* there is system, homogenisation' (Curtis 86). This discussion (one of the most interesting and considered brief examinations of Heaney's language) makes the point that the willed abdication of responsibility for linguistic agency is itself only a trope, part of the poet's deliberate rhetorical strategy. Longley mistrusts the specifically linguistic terms which Heaney imposes on his usage, seeing this imposition as something which occurs 'in default of a specific impulse', and exaggerates the book's 'philological tendency' (Curtis 86). Part of the interest of this comment, I think, is that it is describing the same effect which caused O'Brien to admire the book's direct, unmanipulated presentation of event: Lowell's 'gift of accuracy'.

Like *Wintering Out*, *North* is divided into two major sections, and along the same lines. Part I is a mythopoeic presentation of events and issues in the North, relying for its principal metaphorical device on the parallel of the exhumations from the bogs in Jutland described in P.V. Glob's *The Bog People*. The bog deposits are made to correspond to the surviving elements both of history and of language. Part II, again, is a more personal application of this myth to the actualities of the poet's life, both privately and as public events press in upon it. Again, language becomes both the metaphorical and the real expression of that experience.

The parts are now more clearly subdivided, principally in the longer sequence poems which develop parts of the myth more extensively. In the poems of Part I, the linguistic components of

Irish English (especially in the 'North' of the title) are clearly separated. Thus in a poem like 'Belderg' the linguistic elements which were left unglossed in *Wintering Out* are spelt out:

> So I talked of Mossbawn
> A bogland name. 'But *moss?*'
> He crossed my old home's music
> With older strains of Norse.
> I'd told how its foundation
>
> Was mutable as sound
> And how I could derive
> A forked root from that ground
> And make *bawn* an English fort,
> A planter's walled-in mound,
>
> Or else find sanctuary
> And think of it as Irish . . .
> 'But the Norse ring on your tree?' . . .
>
> . . . in my mind's eye saw
> A world-tree of balanced stones.
> (*N* 14)

This is a well-assembled example of the linguistic mix; in most place-names in Ireland, *bawn is* the Irish word for 'white' or 'fair'. And the operative word in these lines is 'could'; the devoted etymologist can make of place-names what he wants.

Three of the sequences in Part I examine this tripartite composition of the Northern complex more fully again, one by one: Danish, Irish and English (as the etymological components were represented in 'Broagh'). This is the part of the book that Longley accuses of 'homogenisation', finding it unduly pro-grammatic and willed (Curtis 86). 'Viking Dublin: Trial Pieces' deals with the Norse and Danish element; 'Funeral Rites' is concerned with Irish myths, current and past; and 'Bone Dreams' is an etymologically searching metaphor for the way the English language has penetrated the culture, represented at the start by

> White bone found
> on the grazing:
>
> a small ship-burial.
> (*N* 27)

This allusion to Sutton Hoo, or to Scyld's funeral with which *Beowulf* opens (and which Heaney will translate in *The Haw Lantern* as 'A Ship of Death': *HL* 20) introduces the backward push through

> Elizabethan canopies.
> Norman devices,
>
> the erotic mayflowers
> of Provence
> and the ivied latins
> of churchmen
>
> to the scop's
> twang, the iron
> flash of consonants
> cleaving the line.
>   (*N* 28)

One thinks back to the 'release' with which Heaney played on Irish place-names in the *dinnseanchas* poems in *Wintering Out*, showing them to be faithful to the English language as well as to locality – the process is taken a stage further here when the native diction of English provides *ban-hus* to describe any localisation. Robert Welch calls the poem 'a love-poem to *England*' (original emphasis) though his subsequent characterisation as 'Heaney's bony quatrains fired at the English lyric' is more accurate.[22]

This poem takes philological analysis as far as Heaney ever has, extending the phonological model of vowel and consonant to all the 'riches of grammar/ and the declensions', to re-enter memory 'back past/ philology and kennings' in English. now it is the grammatical structure of language itself that is being tested for its adequacy, not its poetic pieties. Indeed, the metaphor here is that the search for language 'adequate to the predicament' digs 'back past' *both* 'philology' (the analysis of language structure itself) *and* 'kennings' (whatever poetic devices, English or Irish, are being used).

This point is strikingly borne out by the collection's first poem (after the two universally admired 'Mossbawn' dedicatory poems). This poem, 'Antaeus', is dated 1966; it is tempting to feel that Heaney has placed it where it is to show how much his formal technique has been pared back in the meantime. Of the poem's ten rhymes, seven are noticeable *deibidhe* ones. And the poem is marked throughout by a tendency to lapse into the 'command of English' clichés of the 'beneath all adult dignity' kind: here we find 'that realm of fame', sand 'that is operative as an elixir', and so on. It offers a heavily prosaic contrast with the spare lucidity and mystery of 'Sunlight'. This is a poem from another age, rather as Yeats's thirty-years-later version of 'The Sorrow of Love' has been thought to sit oddly in the 1890s in the *Collected Poems*;[23] and, of course, as 'A Peacock's Feather' is dated *1972* when it is used in *The Haw Lantern* (*HL* 39).

The second half of *North* is dominated by two long sequences, both manifestoes of a kind: 'Whatever You Say Say Nothing' and 'Singing School'. 'The Ministry of Fear', the first poem in the latter sequence, reconsiders the matter of the place of the Ulster accent and subject within the English lyric, alluding back to Heaney's early poetry, which 'innovated a South Derry rhyme/ With *hushed* and *lulled* for *pushed* and *pulled*' (*N* 64). This displays the same cunning as the *gh* in 'Broagh'. We (the strangers) assume that it is 'pushed' and 'pulled' that have their standard pronunciation, and 'hushed' and 'lulled' that have a non-standard back-rounded sound. But we can't be absolutely sure: it is a cunning example, because hypercorrection (a notorious trap for the dialectally disadvantaged and upwardly mobile) often produces the vowel of standard 'hushed' in 'pushed' (as in 'bull' and 'butcher').

Later in the poem, Heaney summarises the position with startling Harrisonian acerbity:

> Ulster was British, but with no rights on
> The English lyric: all around us, though
> We hadn't named it, the ministry of fear.
>
> (*N* 65)

This is an extreme example of the outspokenness of the second half of *North*, which accordingly reverts to the harshness of diction of Heaney's early poetry, for the newspapermen

> Who proved upon their pulses 'escalate',
> 'Backlash' and 'crack down', 'the provisional wing',
> 'Polarization' and 'long-standing hate'.
>
> (*N* 57)

This is the language of Ulster asserting its 'rights on/ The English lyric', at least according to the journalistic stereotype. Echoing Leopold Bloom again (the same *Ulysses* passage quoted already from 'Traditions' in *Wintering Out*), this stanza of 'Whatever You Say Say Nothing' ends: 'Yet I live here, I live here too, I sing' (*N* 57), going on to parody the conniver 'in civilized outrage' just as tellingly as 'Punishment' had.

The arguments about *North* have centred on poems such as 'Punishment', in the same way that Yeats's 'Chinese curse' employment of mythology was attacked by Conor Cruise O'Brien as politically irresponsible and exploitative of public events.[24] Edna Longley draws on this poem as well as 'Exposure' at the end of the volume to provide the title for her essay on Heaney's politics in Curtis, '"Inner Emigré" or "Artful Voyeur"? Seamus Heaney's *North*'), rephrasing succinctly a question that is central to all Heaney's self-examination throughout the volume. The dilemma was phrased even more closely to O'Brien's Yeats by Dillon Johnston, who called it 'calculated schizophrenia'.[25]

None of these readings seems to give sufficient credit to the self-projection of the poetic persona involved. It was understandable, therefore, that Heaney said before his next volume, *Field Work*, that he was looking forward to being able to use the first-person pronoun to mean himself again. This too, of course, like transparent poetic language, is no more than an ideal, a rhetorical trope. But it is clear that the first person in the poem 'Punishment' is the writer in the abstract; that is, the person who uses suffering or public events to create material: the writer who has always declared the wish to represent the writing self as an example of the experiencing observer. So the judgement in the poem is not a moral or political one; it is an artistic one. Looking at the poem in the light of Glob's book clarifies this; indeed, the accusation in the poem could be extended from the persona to the production of *The Bog People*, the Donatello-like beauty of whose photographs might well be accused of exploitation, if such an accusation is to be levelled at all. Indeed, responsibility for it can be attributed to Glob himself, whose writing, if it is accurately represented by the translation, does seem unduly florid.

Perhaps the principal ambition (and achievement) of *North* can be seen by linking the first and the last poem. 'Sunlight' opens with the mysteriously evocative line 'There was a sunlit absence' (*N* 8), and the poem continues throughout its length to strain to express the mystery of unexpressed domestic love. This is the inarticulacy which tends to be associated with natural goodness: Cordelia's 'I cannot heave/ My heart into my mouth'.[26] But this inability to speak presents difficulties for the literary reporter. Heaney's technique in 'Sunlight' is to use a kind of 'cross-wiring' between different areas of language (which is what happens anyway when an author assigns words, which were not literally spoken, to a character). This complexity is signalled in that first line: the adjective 'sunlit', in standard application, can apply only to objects in which this abstract quality can be said to inhere. It cannot apply to an abstraction. Similar cross-writings occur throughout: 'the wall of each long afternoon', the sun standing against the wall, love like a hidden gleam (a gleam must be seen, if it is to exist at all). Part of the source of this effect may again be in Yeats: for example, the symbolist device at the start of 'The Tower' which attaches 'decrepit age' to the poetic persona 'as to a dog's tail', where the concrete is tied to the abstract by a similar 'cross-wiring'.[27]

All these linguistic effects are attempts, as in the language of the mystic, to express the inexpressible, which in this case is absence. Henry Hart plots *North* particularly convincingly into his scheme of the progress of the mystical *via negativa* from *Door into the Dark* to *The Haw Lantern* (Hart 80), going on (82ff.) to relate this interestingly to the language of the book's poetics.

Corcoran observes the importance of absence as a theme in *North* without making a great deal of it. In the light of Heaney's poetry since *Station Island*, it is tempting to suggest that absence is not the deconstructive idea of deferred explanation but Heaney's characteristic wish that the poem should come into being as a direct expression of objects and events without the intermediacy of the poet: a *topos* not of inexpressibility but of the unexpressed. It might be said that just as *Door into the Dark* set out to explore things hidden both in the psyche and in history, and *Wintering Out* was an attempt to sit out a bad period in history, *North* attempts to chart moral absence, the abdication of the responsibility of judgement.

On the literal (perhaps overliteral) level, this, of course, is also evident as Heaney's absence from Northern Ireland after his move to Wicklow in 1972, away from the poet's 'interesting times', which might confer their paradoxical blessing on him. Such an interpretation is borne out by 'Exposure', the last poem in 'Singing School' and one of Heaney's most effective confessional poems, functioning as an apologia for the whole book. The theme of absence is suggested by the proliferation of non-finite verbal constructions after the finite calendar placing of the first line, 'It is December in Wicklow': 'alders dripping', 'inheriting', 'falling', 'imagining'. None of the poem's events in fact comes to pass: 'A comet that was lost/ Should be visible at sunset' (*N* 72). This is logically as impossible as it is to see the gleam of the scoop sunk in the meal, or to cast sunlight on something that is not there. The crucial question in 'Exposure' is: for what has the poet abandoned the 'once-in-a-lifetime portent'? The lyricism of the absent 'comet's pulsing rose' is a large sacrifice.

But the poem claims this sacrifice as a 'responsible *tristia*', in a phrase I have anticipated several times already. The meagre heat that can be blown up from the sparks in Wicklow is perhaps a suggestion of a more important absence, also suggested by the first poem. Extraordinary events – the comet's pulsing rose (the colour of blood) – also make absent the hidden gleam (Wordsworth's word for visionary insight, as Heaney reminds us elsewhere) of the norms of domestic love and unexpressed affection. In a very Yeatsian phrase ('some who'), he laments in the poem his exposure to 'the anvil brains of some who hate me'. In his next book he attempts to escape the desolating glare of the public self-exposure at the end of *North*.

Field Work

Henry Hart says of the two Parts of *North* that they are poetry- and prose-like respectively (77). This is a good way of characteris-ing the difference; even so, despite its fullness of imagery, the narrow lines (or 'skinny quatrains', as Edna Longley calls them) prevent even Part I from being poetic in any expansive way. In fact, the poetic impulse which is curbed by the severities of *North* is – paradoxically – much more in evidence in the more florid prose poems of *Stations*, written mostly in 1970–71 but published in the same year as *North*, 1975 (the seven pieces from *Stations* anthologised in *New Selected Poems 1966–1987* are placed before the *North* poems). The poetic devices there are typical of Heaney's more open style – for example, the *dinnseanchas* of 'The stations of the west': 'light ascending like its definition over Rannasfast and Errigal, Annaghry and Kincasslagh',[28] and the freed poeticism, which is so far from the language of *North*, in 'Cloistered': 'Light was calloused in the leaded panes of the college chapel and shafted into the terrazzo rink of the sanctuary' (*S* 20), which has a marked whiff of the poet's notebook to it.

By the time of *Field Work* Heaney is declaring his determination to let this more poetic note back into the main corpus: 'to write like a poet for a change', to borrow the words of the 1991 'South Bank Show' Bragg interview about *Seeing Things*. When *Field Work* appears, he quotes a letter to Brian Friel in the important interview with Frank Kinahan: 'I no longer wanted a door into the dark, but a door into the light' (see p. 82, n. 36). He also expresses a yearning to be able to use the first person to refer to himself again (a rebuke, no doubt, to interpreters who had read *North* too biographically, seeing the poet as 'the laureate of violence' or 'the artful voyeur'; but also a wish to be no longer 'absent').

It is clear from everything Heaney said about *Field Work* that he wants, in the new book, to return to something like the 'devil-may-careness' with which he wrote the *Wintering Out* 'place-naming' poems. 'The Tollund Man' had been an attempt to escape the confinements of *that* particular myth of locality, by internationalising his subject: by relocating the *dinnseanchas* in Denmark. He now wants to change again: to some extent, to change back.

With the change, which Deane thought so risky, from the myth of *North* goes a change of form. In the interview with James Randall Heaney says: 'the narrow line was becoming habit. The shortness of a line constricts, in a sense, the breadth of your movement. Of course a formal description is never strictly formal.'[29] The dominant creative metaphor in *North* was the clarity of vision: 'the bleb of the icicle'; now the metaphor is to let the language find its own course and resist co-option.

In evaluating what Deane calls the 'abandoning of a tried and proven myth', we should recall that what Heaney admired most about Yeats was his ability to 'remake himself' by rewriting or by turning to a completely new subject and treatment. 'He bothers you', Heaney writes, 'with the suggestion that if you have managed to do one kind of poem in your own way, you should cast off that way and face into another area of your experience until you have learned a new voice to say that area properly' (*P* 110).

Heaney's intention accordingly to 'remake himself' – to use 'I' to mean himself, or to go through 'a door into the light' – encountered a good deal of resistance. Like Deane, Helen Vendler voices the resistance to the change among Heaney's readers: 'Heaney is the sort of poet who, because he is so accomplished in each stage, is begrudged his new departures; we want more of what so pleased us earlier.'[30]

However, in his determination to move away from the myth and formality of the archaeological drilling stanza, Heaney opens *Field Work* with as programmatic a linguistic statement as 'Fodder' at the start of *Wintering Out*, the strange and powerful 'Oysters'. This opens with a masterly 'Keats and Embarrassment' piece of nerve-jangling, introducing an irritation that runs all through the poem: 'Our shells clacked on the plates' (*FW* 11). But, with an echo of Lewis Carroll's 'The Walrus and the Carpenter' ('Oysters' seems to me to have a Buñuel-like surrealist air which makes this comparison not unapt), the oysters become the passive victims of violence, 'ripped and shucked and scattered'. The pleasant social gathering, 'toasting experience', is spoilt by the association with the exploitative, imperialist Romans hauling damp panniers of oysters south to Rome, as 'the glut of privilege'. The inability to enjoy freedom without such principled reflections makes the speaker angry, and he concludes with active aggression:

> I ate the day
> Deliberately, that its tang
> Might quicken me all into verb, pure verb.
> (*FW* 11)

Of all the linguistic metaphors used by Heaney, this is making the most forceful claim. To see the force of the 'pure verb' we have to recall what was, in the corpus as a whole, the immediately preceding poem, 'Exposure' at the end of *North*. As has been remarked before, that poem is full of non-finite verbal constructions, to express the absence, stasis and depression that followed the poet's missing 'the once-in-a-lifetime portent,/ The comet's pulsing rose' (*N* 73). It hangs on a string of participles and verbal nouns: 'alders *dripping*, birches/ *Inheriting* the last light'; 'falling'; 'imagining'; 'whirled'; 'counselling'; 'weighing and weighing'; 'escaped'; 'taking'; 'feeling'; 'blowing' and 'pulsing' (emphasis added). Helen Vendler had contrasted with this verbal stasis the poem 'Kinship' in *North*, which she called 'a poetry of verbs',[31] quoting

> The mothers of autumn
> sour and sink,
> ferments of hush and leaf
>
> deepen their ochres.
> Mosses come to a head,
> heather unseeds.
>
> (*N* 43)

This, however, is an apparent contrast in part only; most of the verbs here are intransitive. The only formally transitive verb in these lines is reflexive in meaning (and therefore intransitive): the ochre colours deepen *themselves*, rather than being acted upon by 'ferments'. Similarly, 'unseeds' is a kind of anti-verb.

The real contrast comes at the end of 'Oysters', where the movement away from the non-finite and passive could not be more marked than it is in the aggressively transitive government of such a general object as 'the day' by the poet's eating. The 'pure verb' that he wants to 'quicken' into (be made alive by) is linked to the notion of artistic freedom, the obverse of the 'responsible *tristia*' of 'Exposure'.

The treatment of verbs is of enormous importance, both in Heaney's criticism and in his poems, from this point onwards. Verbs are the strongest case of the general movement away from the phonological stress of 'Anahorish' and 'Broagh' towards an employment of metaphors drawn from grammar, which was already evident in such poems as 'Bone Dreams' in *North*, with its 'grammar and declensions' (*N* 28). Corcoran calls this concentration on verbs 'a willed turning outwards from the enclosing, static nouns of earth and myth and placename in which the earlier work had its genesis'.[32] In his book on Heaney (144) he quotes Mandelstam's 'Orioles in the woods' as one important source for Heaney's increasing tendency to use the terms of linguistic analysis in the poetry itself (though the tendency is so much more sustained in Heaney that I think an influence does not need to be suggested):

> Orioles in the woods: length of vowels alone
> makes the metre of the classic lines. No more
> than once a year, though, nature pours out
> the full-drawn length, the verse of Homer.
>
> This day yawns like a caesura.[33]

Heaney's employment of grammatical terminology is much more insistent than the more familiar synaesthetic presentation of the world in terms of poetic rhythm (for the same reason that analysis of the language of poetry has tended in English to be confined to metre rather than grammar and semantics).

This is significant, because Heaney increasingly wants to bring his metalanguage nearer to meaning and reality rather than keeping it to formalities. I stress throughout this book that Heaney's allying of 'phonetics and feeling' is of great importance for the interpretation of his language. However, his allying of grammar and feeling is both more unusual and more crucial for the interpretation of his writing (Yeats's grand formula 'passionate syntax' might be paralleled, although he does much less with it as a critical concept within the poetry than Heaney does[34]).

From *Field Work* on we find the external world described more in terms of noun and verb than of vowel and consonant. The distinction between transitive and intransitive verbs is the most recurrent aspect of this classification. It can be seen as part of a 'chain of being' in verbs, from the finite-active-transitive at the top to non-finite and passive constructions at the bottom. The distinction between transitive and intransitive, as a matter of controlling or not, is implicit but crucial in Heaney's distinction between Wordsworth and Yeats (*P* 61–78). The Wordsworthian child is free because it simply *is*; like any creature in nature, plant or animal, it 'has its being', intransitively. Yeats's natural world, by contrast, is always under control. In the next chapter we will see fully how the aspiration towards Yeatsian control, towards the condition of 'pure verb' (which, like the ideals of tranparency and the unexpressed, is no more than an aspiration), is inevitably doomed to failure in *Station Island*, in poems such as 'In Illo Tempore'. Once again, the fatedness of the aspiration has to be seen in relation to its ethical standing. The imperialism implicit in the Roman parallel in 'Oysters' means that, like several other Dedalus-like bids for freedom in Heaney, it will be frustrated by a regard for public responsibility.

The bid for a new freedom of speech in *Field Work* has metrical as well as grammatical entailments, as is spelt out in the James Randall interview:

> I wrote a fairly constricted freeish kind of verse in *Wintering Out* and *North* in general, and then in the new book *Field Work*, I very deliberately set out to lengthen the line again because the narrow line was becoming habit.... And the rhythmic contract of metre and iambic pentameter and long line implies audience.[35]

What is most striking about this at first glance is the oxymoron it opens with: a verse which was 'constricted' and 'freeish', terms which might be taken as dictionary opposites. The idea is clear enough: formal verse, which is traditional in English, is taken as read, and does not draw attention to itself, leaving the writer free to communicate directly; paradoxically, in the history of English, free verse has been the exception rather than the rule, and thus constricts communication by being remarkable in itself. A similar point has often been made about the formal looseness of Milton's *Samson Agonistes*. By contrast with Heaney's personal form, the artesian stanza of his previously 'enabling myth', he now wants to return to the form which is the general norm for the English lyric because the rhythmic *contract* 'of metre and iambic pentameter and long line' implies an audience (that is, a general audience: not a specialist, local one). The reading audience responds to the normative form as a fulfilment of a social contract. We recall Heaney's saying, in 'Feeling into Words', that the poetic voice was partly his own speaking voice. What this declaration seems to aim at is the discarding of that voice in favour of the social voice of tradition.

Paradoxically, this seems to be a necessary step in 'remaking himself' and using the poetic 'I' to mean himself again. The change has to be achieved on formally neutral ground. Certainly the iambic pentameter is very pronounced in *Field Work*, moving emphatically away from what Heaney said to Frank Kinahan about *North*: 'the musical grace of the English iambic line was some kind of affront. It needed to be wrecked.'[36] It is restored to a prominent position as the 'home key' in *Field Work* – a prominence it never subsequently loses.

The dominant Shakespearian iambic is signalled from the first of the 'Glanmore Sonnets': 'Old ploughsocks gorge the subsoil of each sense' (*FW* 33). Heaney's excellent ear is apparent in his variations on the form (as in Elizabethan sonnet sequences), but the fact that it is the 'home key' is as evident here as it is in them. This virtuoso skill is almost parodied in another variant on *dinnseanchas* in 'Glanmore Sonnet VII', intoning the BBC shipping forecast which plays Chaucerian variations on the iambic pattern, starting off with a run of trochaic inversions – 'Dogger, Rockall, Malin, Irish Sea' (*FW* 39) – and ending with a new set of pieties of place: 'Elsewhere on Minches, Cromarty, The Faroes'. This dazzling performance also includes a couplet marrying Old English kennings with the 'horseback, assback, muleback' of Yeats's 'Lapis Lazuli':

> Of eel-road, seal-road, keel-road, whale-road, raise
> Their wind-compounded keen behind the baize,

before a run of French boat-names to complete the linguistic composite: '*L'Etoile, Le Guillemot, La Belle Hélène*'.

But the metre is not the most striking feature of the language of *Field Work*. Likewise, the metalinguistic commentary is much more incidental than in most Heaney volumes: no more than such commonplaces as 'Wader of assonance' (30), 'neuter . . . loneliness' (12), 'glottal stillness' (49), and the classic Heaney-as-child formulation 'etymologist of roots and graftings' (37). Heaney's declared intention was 'to fortify the quotidian into a work',[37] and there is a marked preponderance (in the terms of Jakobson, used above) of everyday language over the elevated forms specific to poetry or the codes of criticism. The first group of more elevated poems culminates in 'Sibyl' with a voice that sounds like Eliot's 'familiar compound ghost' in 'Little Gidding': '"I think our very form is bound to change"' (*FW* 13). From then on the language draws consistently on everyday diction and the most familiar metrical form, the iambic.

The vernacular is used here, fulfilling the aspiration to work with the quotidian, with almost unprecedented confidence. The dangers of not being read as meant never arise; neither does the developed use of *deibidhe* rhymes present any problems now. In, for example, 'The Harvest Bow' ('dresser/snare'; 'corona/straw'; 'braille/palpable') or 'Casualty' ('too/curfew'; 'held/trembled'); or 'Glanmore Sonnets' I ('years/tractors'; 'sense/redolence'), the rhymes are incorporated as part of Heaney's virtuoso technique. Moreover, the vernacular usages occur at points of tension in what are recognised as the greatest poems in this book of elegies:

> There you used hear guns fired behind the house
> ('The Strand at Lough Beg': *FW* 17)

> 'Now you're supposed to be
> An educated man,'
> I hear him say. 'Puzzle me
> The right answer to that one.'
> ('Casualty': *FW* 23)

> Country voices rose from a cliff-top shelter
> With news of a great litter – 'We'll pet the runt.'
> ('In Memoriam F. Ledwidge': *FW* 59)

The vernacular occurs, too, in less tragic contexts: in 'The Badgers' – which is, in another vein, one of the great poems in the book – the observer stands 'half-lit with whiskey' in the garden (*FW* 25); the poet's wife, horrified by a rat swaying on a briar, urges: 'Go you out to it' (*FW* 41).

There is an obvious connection between the unworked honesty of the vernacular and the figure – mentioned already – of inarticulacy as natural goodness. In one of the essays in *Paddy and Mr Punch*,[38] Roy Foster notes that 'demotic exile literature is an expression, by professional intermediaries, on behalf of the inarticulate – very much in the tradition of Irish ballad poetry'. It also fits the condition of the poets who saw themselves as 'the Dispossessed' (as in the title of *An Duanaire: Poems of the Dispossessed 1600–1900*,[39] the review of which by Heaney is an important essay in *The Government of the Tongue*, 'The Poems of the Dispossessed Repossessed': *GT* 30–5).

For Heaney, this history of imposed inarticulacy coincides productively (and perhaps not accidentally) with the 'famous Ulster reticence'. In *Field Work*, and increasingly afterwards in Heaney, figures of inarticulacy proliferate: in the elegy for Sean Armstrong – 'something in your voice/ Stayed nearly shut (*FW* 20). In 'Casualty', again, the victim orders drinks silently

> By a lifting of the eyes
> And a discreet dumb-show
> Of pulling off the top.
> (*FW* 21)

I have already mentioned the ultimate instance: the hand fingering the harvest bow 'like braille,/ Gleaning the unsaid off the palpable' (*FW* 58).

On the face of it, these figures of the 'unsaid' and the inarticulate sound paradoxical in a book dedicated to the liberation of the poetic voice. But Heaney's poetic voice is, in a way, one of Foster's 'professional intermediaries', giving a voice to the voiceless. After all, what elegy does is to give voice to the terminally voiceless. There are two senses in which this book is elegiac: first the obvious one, that it contains some of the finest elegies in modern English poetry (in an area, incidentally, where modern Irish poetry is particularly strong: for example, Longley, Muldoon and Michael Davitt); but the book is elegiac, too, in its homesickness for Ulster. The figure of the homesick Ulster poet, Sweeney, has been in Heaney's head throughout the 1970s, and the translation of his deracinations will be his next literary project, *Sweeney Astray*.

But the poet homesick for the North is already manifest in a number of ways in *Field Work*: obviously in the vernacular usages quoted above, all of which are as foreign to Southern Irish English as they are to Standard English. But there is also a celebration of Ulster consonantalism, of the kind quoted above from W.R. Rodgers, especially in the poem 'The Singer's House', written for Heaney's friend David Hammond, who is one of the best contemporary Ulster folksingers:

> When they said *Carrickfergus* I could hear
> the frosty echo of saltminers' picks.
> (*FW* 27)

Surely there is resonance for the partially exiled poet in these famously haunting lines from 'The Strand at Lough Beg': as the subject of the poem, Heaney's second cousin Colum McCartney, who was the victim of a random sectarian killing, drives along a distant road, he suffers the fate of Yeats's Irish airman far from Kiltartan, flagged down

> Where you weren't known and far from what you knew:
> The lowland clays and waters of Lough Beg,
> Church Island's spire, its soft treeline of yew.
>
> (*FW* 17)

One of the most telling moments in the 'Station Island' sequence comes when the subject of this poem challenges the poet for putting poetry before family or local piety, in some lines reminiscent of the collocation of violence and art in Dante:

> You were there with poets when you got the word
> and stayed there with them, while your own flesh
> and blood
> was carted to Bellaghy from the Fews.
>
> (*SI* 82)

The poet's defence in *Station Island* is calculatedly wheedling and unconvincing ('they were getting crisis first-hand, Colum'). The real defence is the sympathy in the line which links the poet's situation with the cousin's when he hears the news, 'Where you weren't known and far from what you knew'.

Neil Corcoran says: 'for all its poems of the personal life, *Field Work* retains a large political resonance' (Corcoran 135). It is true, I think, that the declarations of the wish for liberation, both in language and more generally, which Heaney expresses have to be seen in the context of the constraints that he shows attending such liberation. The book ends with the translation of Dante's 'Ugolino': a subject which, apart from its prophetic anticipation of the death by starvation which became such as issue with the IRA hunger-strikers two years later, does not seem to relate closely to its subjects. It is the first instance of Heaney's practice, extended in *Seeing Things*, of marking off the book with an ending of epic weight. The third-to-last poem, 'The Harvest Bow', seems to be

the conclusive statement of the issues that have arisen in the book
(*FW* 58). Central to it is the quotation from Coventry Patmore via
Yeats, *The end of art is peace*.

This is indeed, as the poem says, a suitable motto for the 'frail
device', the straw bow, being a decidedly frail political device
itself. As Neil Corcoran observes, there is an uneasy hint, too, in
the apparent logical entailment 'Peace is the end of art', with a
renewed suggestion of the Brechtian Chinese curse: art lives
parasitically off violence, and the end of that denies it sustenance.
It also brings to mind another familiar declaration in Dante's
Paradiso which sits uneasily in the context of these elegies for the
victims of violence: Piccarda's *e'n la sua volontade è nostra pace*
(in God's will is our peace).[40]

This question has arisen at the end of *Field Work* as a response
principally to 'The Strand at Lough Beg', though to other poems
too: especially, perhaps, 'After a Killing', which considers pessi-
mistically the avowed possibility of turning back to normal life,
away from the duties and troubles of the North, in Wicklow after
the killing of the British ambassador there. As ever in Heaney, the
wish of *An Open Letter* to 'let it go', to 'speak in his own voice'
or 'to write like a poet for a change' will be frustrated. The answer
on this occasion is the charge made by Colum McCartney in
Station Island:

> 'you whitewashed ugliness and drew
> the lovely blinds of the *Purgatorio*
> and saccharined my death with morning dew.'
>
> (*SI* 83)

This is an important instance of the 'professional intermediary',
the poet providing a voice for the 'inarticulate': even giving it a
voice to defeat the poet's licence – 'artistic tact' – by bluntly
calling it 'evasion' (*SI* 83). The poet is not at liberty to write freely
in his own voice, released from answerability to the public event.

To take together the three very different books which have been
the subject of this chapter, merely because they were all published
in the 1970s, is no more than an arbitrary convenience. But they
do – paradoxically, given their differences – have one thing in

common: any one of the three might have been accorded the praise given by Neil Corcoran to *Wintering Out* – that it was the 'seminal single volume of the post-1970 period of English poetry' – according to the linguistic and literary-political tastes of the reader. Indeed, Helen Vendler paid a very similar tribute to *North*, which she called 'one of the few unforgettable single volumes published in English since the modernist era'.[41] This series is eloquent proof of Heaney's success in performing more than once the Yeatsian miracle of 'remaking' his poetic identity.

'The limbo of lost words'

The Sweeney Complex

One of the dominant emotions in *Field Work*, I suggested in Chapter 2, was wistful homesickness for Ulster. In the next two books, the homesick poet is identified with Mad Sweeney, the banished Ulster poet of medieval Irish legend. It is appropriate to take the two volumes *Sweeney Astray* and *Station Island* together, because *Sweeney Astray*'s eponymous central character, 'Heaney's Sweeney' (as nearly all the review headline-writers dubbed it), is an important poetic persona in *Station Island* too. *Sweeney Astray* is a pretty faithful but inventively vernacular rendition of the medieval original, in which Heaney had seen: 'there is something here for me' (*Hibernia* interview with Dennis O'Driscoll).[1] This is clear enough: the Ulster poet who has run foul of clerisy and the Irish high-king in combination, and has been transformed into a bird to flee the length and breadth of Ireland, is clearly a useful self-projection for Heaney post-1972. But even more useful than that text itself is the extrapolated figure of the Sweeney poet used as a mouthpiece in *Station Island*, especially in Part Three, 'Sweeney Redivivus'. This third section has been much admired; the figure of the clerically condemned poet who is forced to live in the traditional romantic poetic realm of birds and trees has been seen as an ideal *alter ego* for Heaney:

> he opened my path to a kingdom
> of such scope and neuter allegiance

my emptiness reigns at its whim.
('The Cleric', *SI* 108)

Before turning to that important projection as it is used in the first and third sections of *Station Island*, I want to consider the prosodic formalities of the *Sweeney* translation in the light of the Irish or English metrical schemes I have been considering. A comparison of the two versions, by Heaney and by Flann O'Brien (and they are both very distinguished translations), shows Heaney once again moving towards traditional English versions of the Irish original, as had very successful predecessors, such as Frank O'Connor and Robin Flower.

This is Flann O'Brien's version of the beginning of one of the most celebrated verses from the poem; it is obvious that O'Brien makes little attempt to scale down the lexical and syntactic foreignness of the original:

Bleating one, little antlers,
O lamenter we like
delightful the clamouring
from your glen you make.[2]

Heaney's version of the same quatrain moves a long way from the heptasyllabic basis of the Old Irish, towards a smooth six-syllabled line with an Elizabethan air to it, pleasing to an ear attuned to English lyric metrics:

Suddenly this bleating
and belling in the glen!
The little timorous stag
like a scared musician.
(*SA* 39)[3]

This regularised metre is consistent with Heaney's principle of metre quoted from the Randall interview, in which he declares a wish to move towards the 'rhythmic contract of ... iambic pentameter and long line' which 'implies audience'.

This is not a turning away from the Irish tradition of the

Sweeney poem. If the poem is to be brought up to date and be useful with a modern application (that is, be 'Sweeney Redivivus'), some of the formal differences of the Old Irish original will have to be forgone in modern English. Not that those formalities are entirely absent: still the *deibidhe* rhyme is used – by now almost a recognisable tune of Heaney's own (as it was in *Field Work*), since he uses the rhyme-scheme not in its native seven-syllable structures but in a familiar English octosyllabic.

> All crossed the sea and here you stand
> who'll never all return from Ireland.
> (*SA* 20)

If any particular metric can be said to be the 'home key' where there is so much variety, it is this standard octosyllabic:

> My hand was locked in Sweeney's hand
> until he heard the loud command
> to battle: Come away and join
> arms with Donal on Moira's plain.
> (*SA* 15)

The transparent regularity of this is particularly evident when it is compared with Flann O'Brien's jagged, broken-up metre and syntax.

The variety of language in *Sweeney Astray* also extends, like the mixed registers and etymologies of the poems in *Wintering Out* and *North*, to embrace English-derived usage in words such as 'thole' (63: a favourite Ulster-derived word of Heaney's which recurs in *Seeing Things* 48). In fact, apart from the extended *dinnseanchas* of the Irish place-names which are obviously a principal component of this wanderings poem, the diction is decidedly plain-style English throughout, in both prose and verse.

As part of the question of artistic freedom versus piety, however, the issue of language has a new prominence in *Station Island*, not least in an important poem in the book's first section, 'Making Strange'. Returning to an old theme and an old term ('strange/stranger'), this poem describes the introduction in the local pub of a visitor with 'travelled intelligence' to a native, 'unshorn and bewildered/ in the tubs of his wellingtons'. (The stranger was Louis Simpson, to whom the poem was originally dedicated; the local 'another' was previously assumed to be the poet's father, though we know now that it was not. See Parker 189, 269.) The poem enacts a confrontation of 'Digging' with the world of the well-formed metrical foot ('speech like the twang of a bowstring'). The problem of communication is resolved by a figure which is a brilliantly exact statement of it: 'a cunning middle voice/ came out of a field across the road/ saying "Be adept and be dialect"'. Michael Allen's characterisation of the proven-ance of this voice as 'rather improbable'[4] is oddly literal, since by this stage it is a familiar practice of Heaney's to introduce a voice which emanates without human agency: the longship in the title-poem of *North* is a comparably far-fetched interlocutor.

The grammatical term 'middle voice' adapted here is an eminently suitable expression of the problem of linguistic and social affiliation. Heaney reverts to it on a number of occasions in *The Government of the Tongue* (see Chapter 5). Particularly significant is its use in the discussion of Auden ('Sounding Auden': *GT* 109–28) to fit into the 'scale of being' of verbs (which I also discussed in Chapter 2). As befits a voice which emerges un-announced from the grass, it is called 'a lurking middle voice' which 'disturbs the grammatical peace of the present participle' (*GT* 123). Perhaps even more significantly, in the chapter on Lowell the 'middle voice' is said to be 'neither dramatic monologue exactly nor confessional lyric: enclosed in quotation marks' (*GT* 143). Like the *gh* in 'Broagh', it is pushed from actual usage towards the less committal metalanguage by metaphorical quota-tion marks. Its implications extend outwards with wide applica-tion to the linguistic resolutions of Heaney's divided loyalties and impulses. This voice holds a middle position in many ways: between Irish and English poetics; between loyalty to parish and to the broad mainstream of literature; between 'doing the decent thing' and the indulgent, 'indecent' freedom of the poetic imagina-tion.

The linguistic sense of the term 'middle voice' (as semi-reflexive) is familiar enough (and Heaney describes it in the Auden essay: *GT* 123), but Heaney adapts it to his purposes with remarkable adeptness (to use his own term). To take vocabulary first: the word 'middle' applies neatly to the mixed diction which is used to mediate between local and standard usage – a recurrent practice in

Heaney, as I have shown. And even if (as I have argued above) it leans towards the standard by virtue of the fact that the middle style has been particularly characteristic of English since the sixteenth century, the mixed usage retains an element of dialect too, both as fidelity to the parish and as Kavanaghesque recognition of it as the source of the poet's strength:

> I found myself driving the stranger
>
> through my own country, adept
> at dialect, reciting my pride
> in all that I knew, that began to make strange
> at that same recitation.
>
> (SI 32–3)

This is a bewildering but appropriate piece of defamiliarisation, recalling Heaney's fondness for paradox amounting almost to oxymoron in his characterisation of formal choices (for instance, the 'constricted freeish' of *North*, discussed in the section on *Field Work* in Chapter 2). What the poet is doing here is attempting to familiarise 'the stranger' with the *gh* in 'Broagh' which, we remember, he finds 'difficult to manage'. But the paradox goes deeper. Dialect should not require adeptness; it should be natural (though I have already anticipated the moment in *The Haw Lantern* when the necessity to resume dialect is the most affecting detail of the poet's relations with his mother in the elegies on her: *HL* 28). But here dialect begins 'to make strange'; the defamiliarising is enacted by the grammatical formation whereby this transitive verb is used intransitively.

Contemporary with these volumes is the 'Open Letter' to Motion and Morrison with which Chapter 1 above started. The full calculated complexity of its form is now plain. When it appeared, the roughness of its form, in a stanza whose hallmark is its metrical virtuosity, was thought puzzling. But the roughness of this version of the Burns stanza is its meaning: the simple countryman's reaction to being called British – and not just British, but the very thing that makes modern British poetry what it is. This stanza is about as virtuoso as W. S. Gilbert's limerick beginning 'There was a young man of St Bede's/ Who was stung on the neck by a wasp':

One a Provo, one a Para,
One Law and Order, one Terror –
It's time to break the cracked mirror
 Of this conceit.
It leads nowhere so why bother
 To work it out?
(stanza 23)

This metrical roughness of the provincial is matched by a crunching return to the long-abandoned harsh diction ('No way, my friends': stanza 18). Clearly, the dialect at which this is adept is a very deliberate challenge to the urbane formalities of the well-wrought poem.

Like the metrical peculiarities of *Death of a Naturalist*, then, this roughened diction has proved something of a hostage to fortune. Heaney deals with the problem as it arises in 'Station Island' in the 'South Bank Show' interview with Bragg: '"Station Island" is a poem of self-accusation' in which 'the sweetness of lyric is refused. . . . It tries to put the boot into lyric', because the form of the sequence is dramatic, not lyrical. It is 'a big container, full of subject matter' which has 'no lyric charm'.[5] From this point onwards Heaney increasingly uses a slack diction, culminating in some of the twelve-line poems of *Seeing Things* (though others are extremely elegantly turned, as I shall illustrate). It was also noted, without always seeing what the effect was, that the language of the ghost-speakers in Part Two displayed the same looseness of form as the 'Open Letter', though this was only one element in a wide range of metrical effects in *Station Island*.

Even Neil Corcoran, Heaney's most dedicated and positive reader, seems to misread the language of poem VII in the 'Station Island' sequence, when he says that 'the dialogue is sometimes very heavy-handed', adding: '"Open up and see what you have got" and "Not that it is any consolation,/ but they were caught" are jaw-breakingly unlikely from people in any kind of passion' (169). Perhaps it is more than coincidence that Corcoran himself descends here from the elegant clarity which is normal in his prose to an oddly clichéd usage. What Heaney is doing again is to suggest that the language of the exchange is not rhetorically recast in the poem, but occurs unprocessed. The interlocutory ghost here, William Strathearn, goes on to reject more elevated language, about forgiveness and circumspection, by saying: 'All that's above my head'. Heaney is using ordinary language as a variation of the practice, noted several times already, according to which the event (here involving a verbal exchange) turns into the poem without intermediacy. The practice is reinforced here by the parallel of the verbal conditions in the *Divine Comedy*. The characters in *Inferno* act with passion, but they speak without it; in accordance with God's will, they answer Dante's requests for information in a clear, informative narrative. Heaney abides by a similar convention. (In passing, it is striking how little the commentators on the 'Station Island' sequence have taken into account the ways in which Heaney's linguistic procedures have been affected by Dantesque parallels.)

In philological terms, of course, 'middle voice' applies more properly in grammar than in vocabulary. Heaney comes close to the strict grammatical sense of the term 'middle voice' in Greek (applied by analogy to the description of reflexivity in the verb in some Germanic languages, such as Icelandic), to mean reciprocal or reflexive. The exact function of the middle voice is notoriously hard to tie down, but this is all the more suitable for Heaney's purposes – to apply verbally to a state of action somewhere in the middle between the active and the passive. It is a far remove from the 'verb, pure verb' to which he aspired in 'Oysters' at the start of *Field Work*, with its connotations of resolved and independent action on the writer's part.

As we have seen, and will see again, Heaney is making play with 'medial' conditions of the verb which come between active and passive, transitive and intransitive, and between indicative and subjunctive. Thus, some poems turn again to the grammatical figuration noted above in *Field Work*; its most marked occurrence of all comes in 'In Illo Tempore', a poem which transmutes experience almost totally into language:

> Intransitively we would assist,
> confess, receive. The verbs
> assumed us. We adored.

> And we lifted our eyes to the nouns . . .
> the word rubric itself a bloodshot sunset.
>   (*SI* 118)

The strangely mixed phrase 'lifted our eyes to the nouns' is a good introduction to what is most characteristic of the language of *Station Island*, by contrast with the drive towards the active and verbal in the immediately preceding work. The phrase is 'mixed' in the same way as 'ate the day' in 'Oysters': the material transitive verb 'ate' cannot take the abstract 'day' as object; neither can you look up at a grammatical term, 'the nouns'. Like the inactive middle voice, language seems to lack human agency, appearing to inhere in objects before it is given conscious shaping; as Heaney says of translation more than once, it is 'given' rather than achieved (for example, in the last line of 'Station Island' VI: 'Translated, given, under the oak tree': *SI* 76). Noun-based language is striking throughout *Station Island*, to be linked, perhaps, with Heaney's much-favoured quotation from Michael McLaverty: 'Description is revelation' (*N* 71). Without labouring his methodology, it is tempting to recall Chomsky's theory that all words are at root nouns or verbs: words of description or of action.

Station Island has moved away from *Field Work*'s aspiration towards action. But we must remember that what 'action' means in a Heaney poem is independence of utterance. In the same metaphorical scheme, the noun is a symbol of domination: of what is looked up to ('In Illo Tempore': *SI* 118) and what is irresistible. In the elegies of *Field Work* it was no more than a rhetorical aspiration, of course. But in *Station Island* even the aspiration has gone. Indeed, the very spirit of frustrated anger in which Heaney expresses the desire to be 'quickened into verb' implies that it is an impossibility.

As I have been saying, the linguistic focus in *Station Island* shifts from the verb to the noun in keeping with the shift from an emphasis on 'lyric freedom' back to subject matter in its 'big container', as Heaney characterised the book in the Bragg interview. Just as in *North* the ostensible aspiration to write with the clarity of 'the bleb of the icicle' led to the adoption of a language which was less disposed to scrutinise its own workings, in *Station Island* the weight of the Dantesque theme and the imagistic possibilities of the imaginative world force linguistic examination to one side. But there are two important new linguistic developments. The first is mirrored by the new concentration on noun and non-finite verbal constructions; it might be described as a materialist, rather than a dynamic, aesthetic. Though it lacks its heaviness, it is in some ways a return to the externality of the world of *Death of a Naturalist*. In retrospect from the Bragg interview, Heaney chooses to regard its noun-dominated world as an admission of artistic defeat, in personal terms. The second – which is particularly prominent in the poems of Part Three, and continues to be central in the earlier poems of *The Haw Lantern* – is a turning away from spoken language (and in its rawest form) towards the written. At this stage Heaney may seem to be moving towards an anti-logocentric aesthetic, as Hart suggests, 'to celebrate the concrete accomplishment of writing over the evanscence of speech' (Hart 38). But in the event, Heaney shows that written forms share the inarticulacy of the spoken, especially in the 'Sweeney Redivivus' section.

I have already quoted Heaney's remark that 'up to *North*, that was one book', in the light of which readers have been ready to follow his lead in regarding *Field Work*, with its claimed artistic freedoms, as a new departure, formally and otherwise. Oddly, the much more marked shift in *Station Island* seems to have been less recognised. The formal changes are very striking: towards a language which is rarely rhymed (it is the only book of Heaney's in which the question of Irish forms seems hardly to arise at all), as well as being a good deal denser and more cryptic than anything before or after it.

The heading to this chapter, 'the limbo of lost words', is the last line of the opening of the very important Dantesque poem 'The Loaning', which can be read as the programme for the whole volume and an explanation of its changes. The first sentence is a clear example of the adept dialect that involves rough diction ('an old one') and local usage ('loaning'):

> As I went down the loaning
> the wind shifting in the hedge was like
> an old one's whistling speech. And I knew
> I was in the limbo of lost words.
>
> (*SI* 51)

Although we can imagine what those lost words might be, there cannot be examples of them *because* they are lost. Their local provenance is clear enough: the world of farming childhood.

> They had flown there from raftered sheds and crossroads,
> from the shelter of gable ends and turned-up carts.
> I saw them streaming out of birch-white throats
> and fluttering above iron bedsteads
>
> (*SI* 51)

This section of the poem ends with the book's rationale: these flying words had risen up 'and settled in the uvulae of stones/ and the soft lungs of the hawthorn' (*SI* 51).

This is the furthest Heaney ever goes in claiming that the poem is the unmediated product of the thing itself, as an extension of what Edna Longley called 'Heaney's phonetic fantasy' in discussing 'Viking Pieces' in *North* – the longship's hull 'spined and plosive/ as *Dublin*' (Curtis 86). Even the human articulators (the lungs and the uvula) are transferred to the objects that give rise to the poem. It is strange that Longley says this process 'drives a huge wedge between word and thing'; although it could be accused of driving a wedge between word and speaker, what it does ostensibly is to close the gap between word and thing. Its production is not only a physiological process; it is a physical one. Speech is treated as a product of the natural world of objects rather than of human will, recalling Frost's phrase 'the sound of sense' with which Heaney begins the Plath essay in *The Government of the Tongue* (148). This aesthetic of the material is operative throughout the book, from the '*articulated* twigs' in 'Away from it All' to the '*acoustic* of frost' in 'The First Flight' (emphases added). The confirmation by words rather than experience is at its most forceful in 'the Birthplace', in which the visit to Hardy's birthplace is trawled for poetic material. The nouns – especially, once again, the trochaic compound ones – are turned over like stones in the palm:

> *birthplace, roofbeam, whitewash,*
> *flagstone, hearth,*
> like unstacked iron weights.
>
> (*SI* 35)

The poem concludes with an extraordinary declaration of the priority of writing and verbal form over event. Thirty years ago Heaney read through the night to finish *The Return of the Native*, coming back from the book to a factual reality which is not necessarily more real than the fictional events: not only spoken language but the reality it refers to loses its signifying priority over the written:

> The corncrake in the aftergrass
>
> verified himself, and I heard
> roosters and dogs, the very same
> as if he had written them.
>
> *(SI* 35)

We should not fail to note the Irish colloquialism, 'the very same', with which Heaney quietly reclaims responsibility for the poem.

It is easy to illustrate the prominence of the materially solid elsewhere in this book which founds its sense of reality in the named. One of the most beautiful and cryptic of the poems in the 'Station Island' sequence begins with a run of naming compounds which (like the names for the hare in 'Squarings' *xliii* in *Seeing Things*) are the book's most favoured form:

> Freckle-face, fox-head, pod of the broom,
> Catkin-pixie, little fern-swish.
>
> *(SI* 75)

But from the 'honeymooning, moonlighting' of the opening poem, the book is full of compounds, verbal forms which are, of course, more characteristic of English than of Irish (as in 'Bone Dreams' in *North*, considered above). Here the association of the noun with dominance links to images of English cultural dominance, in the same way that controlling masculinity is associated with English and subservient femininity with Irish.

It is hard to generalise about the language of the central 'Station Island' sequence, at least in the terms which are the guidelines in this book, for two reasons. First, it features a wide variety of metrical forms and styles. Secondly – and more importantly – the Dantesque structure pulls Heaney towards the adoption of *terza rima*, a form which is clearly foreign to the conventions of English and Irish lyric alike. Here, for the last time (because it does not arise in Heaney's later work, where there are different, more colloquial linguistic hostages to fortune), I want to dwell on

Heaney's 'middle voice' practice, which has caused him to be misunderstood all the way from 'Digging' through 'An Open Letter' to these *terza rima* versions.

Heaney's *terza rima* seems to me to be his most impressive achievement in poetic form (comparable with his more generally recognised lexical achievements in terms of evocation and description), both in the twelve-line 'sonnets' of *Seeing Things* and in the five sections of the 'Station Island' sequence. Neil Corcoran tries to comfort the poet for what he sees as his difficulty with the form, noting that it 'is notoriously difficult in English'. Still he adds:

> Heaney's variations on it are bound to summon much too closely for comfort Eliot's tremendous imitative approximation of it in the second section of 'Little Gidding', and Yeats's use of it in a poem Heaney admires in *Preoccupations*, 'Cuchulain Comforted'. (Corcoran 169)

Great as these predecessors are, I think Heaney's *terza rima* in the sequence will come to be regarded as an equally impressive adaptation of the form to his particular purposes. Indeed, the way speech is adapted into the form is much closer to Dante's practice (to the asperity of style he was accused of, the *selvaggia* quality of *Inferno* I, 5 admired by Heaney in 'Envies and Identifications' and noted by Stan Smith in linking Heaney's view of Dante with *De Vulgari Eloquentia*[6]) than anything in the Yeats or Eliot sections, for all the musical urbanity of the section of 'Little Gidding'. Heaney is not concerned, after all, 'To purify the dialect of the tribe' but to incorporate local usage, unpurified, into the literary dialect:

> 'I remember the stale smell
>
> of cooked meat or something coming through
> as I went to open up. From then on
> you know as much about it as I do.'
>
> (*SI* 79)

An even more daring variation on the form is the short line in this stanza of the Carleton section:

> 'O holy Jesus Christ, does nothing change?'

> His head jerked sharply side to side and up
> like a diver surfacing.
>
> (*SI* 64)

The deliberateness of these fractured forms is confirmed by the fact that Heaney's practice has Eliot's in mind when it wants to. The end of the Strathearn apparition – 'and he trembled like a heatwave and faded' (*SI* 80) – is a reworking of Eliot's 'and faded on the blowing of the horn',[7] which in turn is a modernisation of the form of a canto's typical last line in *Inferno*. Eliot and Yeats are following Dante; Heaney is following Dante, Eliot, Yeats and Lowell, as well as using more modern language. The *terza rima* in 'Little Gidding' may be 'tremendous', but it is not the language of the modern era: for example, 'Before the urban dawn wind unresisting'[8] belongs to the seventeenth century. Likewise, Yeats's grave and beautiful version of Dante's form in 'Cuchulain Comforted' is faithful to the letter rather than the spirit of Dante (and accordingly more anachronistic) than Heaney's.

But in Part Three of *Station Island* Yeats is an important presence again, particularly in the group of rather animist tree-poems with which it opens. In three consecutive poems Heaney pays tribute to the master in poems which link, as Yeats does, bird, poet and tree. 'In the Beech' alludes unmistakeably to the chestnut, the 'great-rooted blossomer' at the end of 'Among School Children'. The tree-questioning lines

> And the tree itself a strangeness and a comfort,
> as much a column as a bole. The very ivy
> puzzled its milk-tooth frills and tapers
> over the grain: was it bark or masonry?
>
> (*SI* 100)

inevitably recall 'Are you the leaf, the blossom or the bole?'[9] The next poem, 'The First Kingdom', uses the Yeatsian phrase 'breed and generation', as well as formally recalling the 'horseback, assback, muleback' of 'Lapis Lazuli' in 'cartful, barrowful and bucketful' (*SI* 101). And the following poem uses the Yeatsian gerund 'hosting' as well as a phonic echo in 'new rungs of the air' (of 'brute blood of the air', for example).[10] It is obvious that Yeats's *Last Poems* are a major influence on any destabilising register in poets who are aware of him; the linguistic profligacy and recklessness of a poem like 'High Talk' are just as influential on Yeats's followers as his themes or more regular forms.

'Lapis Lazuli' and 'Among School Children' are two of Yeats's most important 'art or life' poems. This dilemma – which was a natural one for Heaney to face in his era in Northern Ireland, and explicit at least since 'The Harvest Bow' – is an important link with Yeats. On reading 'Yeats as an Example?' from *Preoccupations* now, it seems that Heaney – probably subconsciously – has partly suppressed the ways in which Yeats has been exemplary for him. *Station Island* appeared in 1984 when Heaney was 45; we remember that in the 1978 essay on Yeats's influence he says that Yeats is 'the ideal example for a poet approaching middle age' (*P* 110). This is because he has a devotion to an art founded on life, a devotion which is put forward by that stage of life with unapologetic 'arrogance'. We should not be surprised, then, to find echoes of Yeats in the poetry of this period of Heaney's writing, though there is very little arrogance in the wild 'Sweeney Redivivus' poems of Part Three. One might conjecture that the absence of a Yeats ghost from the cast in the 'Station Island' sequence is attributable to his presence in such a role as part of the 'familiar compound ghost' of 'Little Gidding'.

Certainly, as far as the language and style of *Station Island* are concerned, Yeats is a likelier presence than the severe Joyce of the last poem in the sequence. Beyond the echoes I have noticed, there are other Yeatsian effects in Heaney. One of them brings us back to Kavanagh: the risky or 'chancy' successes Heaney admired in poems such as 'Kerr's Ass'. He quotes the wonderfully funny and malicious passage mocking Yeats's fur coat from George Moore's *Hail and Farewell*,[11] suggesting that this tribute to Yeats's attitude-striking was 'finally more of a testimony to Yeats's genius than a worrier of it' (*P* 107). It is like Auden 'setting [Yeats's] silliness in relation to the gift' (*P* 108). What is clear here is Heaney's acceptance that poetic success can – and maybe must – run the risk of being charged with 'silliness', as Yeats was by Auden and Winters. This is true in two ways: it may actually be successful while also portentous and overreaching (like Yeats's 'eat/ A crazy salad with their meat'[12]); and novel impact may need to be near to the boundary of the embarrassing, as in Ricks's theory of 'Keats and Embarrassment'.

Heaney also runs these risks in the course of offering himself as an exemplary poet: for example, in the self-mockery of 'An Afterwards' in *Field Work*, the dream of posthumousness in which he is approached by Virgil's wife and his own, he puts to his wife the unmistakeably comic Irish, Flann O'Brien-like question:

> 'My sweet, who wears the bays
> In our green land above, whose is the life
>
> Most dedicated and exemplary?'
>
> (*FW* 44)

and receives an answer which rejects 'the sulphurous news of poets and poetry'. Throughout his career, as I have been arguing, he has run the risk of having his language misunderstood as he exploits unstable registers (like the grandiosely inflated one here) to create his own voice. But it is his view, as it was Yeats's (for example, in another poem Heaney greatly admires, 'A Dialogue of Self and Soul'), that a new language cannot be created without running this risk:

> How in the name of Heaven can he escape
> That defiling and disfigured shape
> The mirror of malicious eyes
> Casts upon his eyes until at last
> He thinks that shape must be his shape? . . .
>
> I am content to live it all again
> And yet again, if it be life to pitch
> Into the frog-spawn of a blind man's ditch.[13]

It is an aesthetic which admires the opening of Kavanagh's 'Kerr's Ass':

> We borrowed the loan of Kerr's big ass
> To go to Dundalk with butter.

But it is precisely the smirk-risk of that opening that makes possible Kavanagh's transcendent conclusion:

> And the God of imagination waking
> In a Mucker fog.[14]

Kavanagh's rural rawness was the subject of a sympathetic (but also 'silly') defence against the malice of literary Dublin in an early issue of *The Honest Ulsterman*.[15] Flann O'Brien – a highly gifted heir to George Moore's satirical malice – gave great offence to the champions of Kavanagh by pretending to misread the wonderful poem 'Spraying the Potatoes' as a metaphor for laundering money (interpreting 'potatoes' in the Runyon slang sense of 'capital'). Heaney, of course, is also running the risk of collocation with that most formidably hilarious mocker's *At Swim-Two-Birds* in *Sweeney Astray*, and the Sweeney persona poems in Part Three of *Station Island*.

At Swim-Two-Birds, in its three interlacing narratives, is a striking example of the running together of the three Jakobson languages: the everyday, the exalted and the critical. Its account of Sweeney is intercut with more vernacular matter. For example, this passage, following one of the most heartfelt of O'Brien's own translations of the medieval original, the great verse beginning 'Terrible is my plight this night', refuses to respect the epic scope of Sweeney's leaps:

> – Come here, said Lamont, what's this about jumps?
> – Hopping around, you know, said Furriskey.
> – The story, said learned Shanahan in a learned explanatory manner, is about this fellow Sweeny that argued the toss with the clergy and came off second-best at the wind-up. There was a curse – a malediction – put down in the book against him. The upshot is that your man becomes a bloody bird.
> – I see, said Lamont.
> – Do you see it, Mr Furriskey, said Shanahan. What happens? He is changed into a bird for his pains and he could go from here to Carlow in one hop.[16]

We recall Yeats's lines in 'Nineteen Hundred and Nineteen', written, no doubt, with Moore in mind:

> Mock mockers after that
> That would not lift a hand maybe
> To help good, wise or great
> To bar that foul storm out, for we
> Traffic in mockery.[17]

Heaney is always conscious of the Irish writer's need to be able to traffic in mockery as part of his refusal to exclude the colloquial from more solemn registers. There is no unmockable solemnity. Maybe it is Heaney's rural ancestors (noted in the Preface) who see to that. Of Yeats's 'silliness', Heaney says: 'the silliness of the behaviour is continuous with the sumptuousness of the poetry of the middle period' (*P* 108). This is an important principle, because again and again throughout his career, as we have seen, Heaney's touches of lavish diction or rough metrics have been misread as stylistic flaws. His notion of taste works according to a less inflexible dictate than his most solemn critics have espoused. But, like Kavanagh's risks and Yeats's excesses, the mixed language of the 'middle voice' is central to Heaney's technique.

There is one final aspect of the language of *Station Island* to consider, and it is probably the most important. Moreover, it is the aspect that is carried over most explicitly to *The Haw Lantern*, especially its programmatic opening poem, 'Alphabets': the developed concern, mentioned above, with written rather than spoken language which is so marked a shift in the 'Sweeney Redivivus' section. It means that Heaney is moving away from the predominantly phonological myth of 'Broagh' the 'phonetic fantasy', towards what linguists sometimes call a more 'scriptist' form: language as it is learnt by writing and reading.

This scriptist metaphor has been implicit in the language of earlier parts of the book: the telegraph lines in 'The Railway Children', for example: 'Like lovely freehand they curved for miles' (*SI* 45). Along with this goes a tendency towards quotations which 'start to rise// like rehearsed alibis' ('Away from it All': *SI* 16) and the consequent growth in italicisation. Obviously there is such textual cross-reference to the Sweeney myth and in the revenants of the 'Station Island' sequence; but in addition the book contains quotations from or references to Greek myth, Hansel and Gretel, the Bible, the Church liturgy and catechism, Milosz, Chekhov, Dante, *Hamlet*, Brian Moore's *Catholics*, Hardy, Daniel Corkery, Joyce, E. Nesbit, Paul Muldoon, John Montague, T.S. Eliot, and no doubt more. The inference is that this book is founded as much in written learning as in experience.

If we had to name a single theme as central in it, it would be not the afterlife but nostalgia and loss. Heaney's Midas touch with imagery (Foster's 'axiomatic rightness') is at its finest in some of the elegiac figures of irretrievability here:

> What guarantees things keeping
> if a railway can be lifted
> like a long briar out of ditch growth?
>   ('Iron Spike': *SI* 23)

The same image occurs with a more explicitly linguistic applica-
tion in 'The King of the Ditchbacks':

> As if a trespasser
> unbolted a forgotten gate
> and ripped the growth
> tangling its lower bars –
>
> just beyond the hedge
> he has opened a dark morse.
>   (*SI* 56)

The theme is summarised in 'What the Brick Keeps', the fourth
section of another important statement poem, 'The Sandpit'.
Experience and history in the building industry are represented
here by an idea drawn from the notion of literary canon, in
particular the Eliot conception of tradition. It is suggested that the
physical building holds within it, implicitly waiting to be decoded,
all the human agency that was involved in its production:

> His touch, his daydream of the tanks,
> his point of vantage on the scaffolding
> over chimneys and close hills at noontime . . .
> with one chop of the trowel he sent it all
> into the brick for ever.
> It has not stopped travelling in
> in the van of all that followed.
>
>   (*SI* 55)

As far as we can be sure in the present state of scientific
knowledge, this information is not contained in a recoverable way
within worked materials. But it is an extreme statement of the
priority of the inscribed over the empirical. It recalls the great
statement of another literal impossibility in 'The Harvest Bow':
'Gleaning the unsaid off the palpable' (*FW* 58). More obviously,

of course, it recalls the digging down for evidence in the 'Bog' poems. 'What the Brick Keeps' is overground archaeology.

This concern, which is ultimately elegiac, with the retrievability of lived experience through writing underlies the poems about writing in Part Three of *Station Island*. The procedure is prepared for almost laboriously in the short first poem, 'The First Gloss':

> Take hold of the shaft of the pen.
> Subscribe to the first step taken
> from a justified line
> into the margin.
>
> (*SI* 97)

This is all metaphorical to a degree that might be better described as punning; the shaft of the pen is a conscious reversion to the spade in 'Digging', and the verb 'subscribe' is used to sustain the same metaphor. (Stan Smith says it means here 'paying one's dues, accepting a lineage and an authority'.[18] If this is right, the poem describes the marginalisation of the writer.) Obedience to Joyce's advice not to be hidebound by always 'doing the decent thing' is declared metaphorically by 'the first step taken/ from a justified line'. 'To the margin' fits Sweeney's social condition.

When Heaney said of *Buile Suibhne* in the interview with Dennis O'Driscoll 'There's something here for me',[19] it was clear enough what the congruity was for his experience as displaced Northern poet. But there is a further application of the mythic story which, in a way, has elements of the child's fairytale. One of the most effective parts of the story comes in the later stages of Sweeney's exile, when his wish to return to the warmth and protection of his own people is defeated by the reimposition of the cleric's curse:

> – All the same, Sweeney said, even if Donal, son of Aodh, were to kill me, I will still go to Dal-Arie and trust to the mercy of my own people . . . Then a glimmer of reason came back to him and he set out for his own country, ready to settle there and entrust himself to the people. (*SA* 64)

It is this dependent attachment that makes Sweeney a suitable figure for the displaced Ulster poet, as well as the learning child in the early poems of Part Three. The experience of the mad birdman in the trees is collocated with the child's in his 'tree of knowledge' (*SI* 100). The child learns to read the world as Sweeney learns to read (and distrust) his neighbours on his travels through Ireland, finding himself in the title-poem of this part of the book,

> incredible to myself,
> among people far too eager to believe me
> and my story, even if it happened to be true.
> (*SI* 98)

This idea, which is equally true of a child's experience of parents and of all people who welcome the renegade, is repeated in 'The First Kingdom', where the unspecified 'they' are said to be 'two-faced and accommodating'.

In his review of *Sweeney Astray* in *The Sunday Times*, John Carey said that Heaney's principal characteristic was doubt.[20] This is borne out in these poems, full of images of unbelief, homesickness and elegiac uncertainty. The last word is 'exhaustion', the culmination of a series of similarly unfulfilled endwords: 'inestimable'; 'emptiness'; 'disbelief'; 'demeaned'; 'preCopernican night'. This disposition is linked to the theme of the difficulty of interpreting language, encapsulated in 'Holly': 'I reach for a book like a doubter' (*SI* 115). The teachers in this school are unusually devoid of charm: the prowling 'Hermit' (109); 'the Master', with 'his book of withholding' (110); the 'jealous art' of the snarling 'Scribes' (111). The images from writing are similarly charmless: the scribes' 'rumps of lettering'; 'the old rules/ we all had inscribed on our slates'; the overbearing cleric's 'parchments and scheming', with his 'cramp-jawed abbesses' and 'his Latin and blather of love'. No doubt these are all to be heard in the voice of the exiled Sweeney, but it is impossible not to contrast this cross and dusty bookishness with the evocativeness of the aural images: the seabirds' 'cry in the small hours' and 'the acoustic of frost'. It is true that Heaney turns his linguistic attentions in *Station Island* from spoken to written forms, but only to demonstrate the unsatisfactoriness of the latter. This realm, where words have lost the magic of their sounds and the written language has not yet achieved emotional effectiveness, is indeed a Limbo, at best. From its first poem onwards, the next book will attempt to re-create the written language by going back to its sources.

Beyond the Alphabet

The Haw Lantern *and* Seeing Things

As I have been noting along the way, various stages in Heaney's development have been said to mark a new direction. 'The Tollund Man' and the Glob-influenced poems of *Wintering Out* were a marked departure in theme from what preceded them, with a corresponding change in forms, and in my Introduction I see *North* as the beginning of Heaney's middle period (though this will no doubt come to seem a premature division, since he was in his early thirties when the poems of *North* were being written). After *North*, Helen Vendler and Seamus Deane paid tribute to the courage involved in the abandonment of the highly successful myth of drilling into the prehistory of terrain and language with the 'skinny stanza' (Edna Longley) of 'artesian quatrains' (Blake Morrison and others).[1] Heaney himself lent support to this view that *Field Work* was a new departure, with its longer lines more amenable to audience, saying: 'Up to *North*, that was one book'.

From our later vantage point, there are other ways of seeing the matter. Some of the individual volumes seem to have a higher profile, with the others no more than intermediary stages filling out developments which can be more clearly seen in those higher-profiled books. According to this view, the prominent books are *Death of a Naturalist*, *North* (perhaps co-opting some of *Wintering Out*, which was said to have been published at a medial stage so that some of its tendencies remained inchoate, to be brought to fulfilment in *North*) and *Station Island*.

Heaney's two books since *Station Island* have been considered hard to place. *The Haw Lantern* was seen as a highly effective and affecting book of personal poems which turned inward the major focus of its predecessor with a loss of power and a rather mandarin slightness. And although *Seeing Things* clearly marked new developments in a number of ways, there has been no consensus about its height of profile either. Indeed, there was less consensus about its reception altogether than about any previous book of Heaney's. This critical indefiniteness is betrayed even in one of the most enthusiastic tributes to the book, by Peter Levi, who wrote: 'From this stage onwards there is no possible rivalry. He must pace himself.'[2] The problem is that it is not easy for the commentator to evaluate the performance of the athlete who has to pace himself.

In such a quandary the poet's self-commentary will obviously assume great importance. In Chapter 5 below I will attempt to give a general description of Heaney's theory of lyric form, mainly as it was articulated in *The Government of the Tongue*, relating it to Dante who, for all his extensive epic geometry, is Heaney's model of the lyric writer. But before that I want to consider whether the analysis of Heaney's poetic language and the linguistic commentary incorporated in the poems can be used to resolve this dilemma of placing the two most recent volumes.

The Haw Lantern

There have been some confident judgements on *The Haw Lantern*. In the most widely reproduced review of it, Michael Allen began with mathematical assurance:

> Between half a dozen and a dozen poems in *The Haw Lantern* are very fine, have a kind of imaginative inevitability. (This is a high score for most slim volumes but low for Heaney.)[3]

This seems not altogether enlightening, and somewhat grudging, coming from the man so handsomely acknowledged by Heaney in the Foreword to *Preoccupations* as 'the reader over my shoulder' (*P* 14).

The most confident overall reading of the book is Henry Hart's; he calls it Heaney's 'most sustained attack on the binary oppositions that have stratified and oppressed his society in the past, tracing them, as Jacques Derrida and others have done, back to the Platonic and Judeo-Christian origins of Western civilization' (Hart 7). This grand and precise strategy sounds interesting, but it proves hard, even in Hart's own mystical terms, to show it to be true of *The Haw Lantern* as a whole. Heaney's objective, Hart goes on to say, is 'to affirm the productive interplay of differences (Hart 7); and there are moments in the book where this *does* seem to be central – in the concern with dialect and inexpressiveness in some of the 'Clearances' sonnets, for example; but the book cannot seriously be said to have any such overall programme.

Stan Smith, hardly less grandly, sees the whole volume as concerned with the learning of all language as a symbolic and analogical system of representation, beginning with the father's hands shadowing a rabbit on the wall.[4] Certainly, such a system of general representation is wonderfully figured in the book's dedicatory couplet, to Bernard and Jane MacCabe:

> The riverbed, dried-up, half-full of leaves.

> Us, listening to a river in the trees.

We recognise the 'dried-up source' of the last poem in *Station Island*, which demands a 'book of changes' (*SI* 121). This couplet introduces such a book of changes: the old springs of eloquence, as in 'Personal Helicon', are drying up for the time being (they will be reopened in *Seeing Things*); but the source of inspiration is still to be found, transfigured, in the trees. The figurative 'river in the trees' represents an imagined version of the experienced reality, like writing. The medieval term for this would be 'anagogical'; it signals, in Hart's terms. an upward move towards the transcendental, which will require a relearnt language.

It is not surprising, then, that *The Haw Lantern* begins (as, of course, Hart says) with a declared shift towards writing as the linguistic topic. *The Haw Lantern* resembles several of its predecessor volumes in beginning with a poem which considers linguistic issues expressly in a kind of manifesto: earlier examples were 'Fodder' (*WO*) and 'Oysters' (*FW*). The first poem in *The Haw Lantern*, 'Alphabets', links back more specifically to 'Digging' (*DN*.) In Chapter 3 we noted how the turn towards written language in Part Three of *Station Island* was linked (as 'Digging' was partly) with the child's language acquisition, seen in terms of Sweeney's bird's-eye view. 'Alphabets' begins with something to which logocentric linguistic theory has given less attention: the stages of the child's acquisition of *written* language.

'Alphabets' tackles this in a decidedly ambitious way, with an overview of linguistic development as, like a telescoped Joycean *Portrait of the Artist as a Young Man*, it aims to chart in its three sections the salient stages of written linguistic development: the child's first encounter with symbolic written forms, such as 'the forked stick that they call a Y'; then the more learned stage of school-learning that moves from the encounter with Latin, 'marbled and minatory', to Celtic manuscript illustration, described in familiar Heaney imagery: 'The lines of script like briars coiled in ditches' (*HL* 2). Finally, the poem's ostensibly unidentified 'he' is lecturing at Harvard, 'alluding' to Shakespeare and Graves (the repeated verb no doubt draws on its etymology, *ludum* – a game – as self-deflation). But this last section recapitulates in non-innocent terms the first stage of learning, now in learned linguistic forms (recalling Heaney's opposing of Montague's learned landscape to Kavanagh's innocent), drawing on Latin and space travel. The innocent/learned opposition is resolved in favour of the innocent in the poem's wonderful closing quatrain:

> Or like my own wide pre-reflective stare
> All agog at the plasterer on his ladder
> Skimming our gable and writing our name there
> With his trowel point, letter by strange letter.
> (*HL* 3)

All that has been learned in the elaborate educational process which has enabled the maturing user of language to 'allude' to Shakespeare and Graves is a metaphorical terminology: the ability to verbalise the shape of the potato-pit's mouth as a 'delta'. It is a retrospective application of Greek learning to what had been known anyway.

The poem comes close to saying that language is an affectation which adds nothing to experience. McLaverty's statement – much favoured by Heaney – that 'description is revelation' is true of the mind's description rather than the written symbol's tidying-up process. The end of 'Alphabets' suggests that revelation comes from observation of the magic in things rather than the ability to assign language to them. Throughout his next two books Heaney will be concerned with the poetic endeavour to represent what, in *Seeing Things*, he calls, 'credit[ing] marvels'. In this project the elements of the alphabet have obvious limitations.

This is by no means *The Haw Lantern*'s sole subject; indeed, as a volume it is less single-minded than any of Heaney's others. It is split in immediately striking ways. As its blurb says, it contains 'exercises in an allegorical vein' that are surprising in the light of Heaney's development up to that point. This rather self-conscious, Kafkaesque series of coded semi-public poems is Heaney's most abstract work: very different from the book's other principal element, the series of eight sonnets in tribute to his recently dead mother, which are as concrete as he ever gets. Predictably, the language used for each section, and the linguistic issues each has to address, are very different too. But what they do have in common is the sense, already present in 'Alphabets', of the limitation of learned written forms.

'Clearances', the sonnets in memory of his mother, are some of Heaney's most admired poems. Nobody would dispute Michael Allen's judgement that 'sonnets 2 and 3 . . . are . . . certain to sit in the anthologies of the twenty-third century . . . with comparable poems by Vaughan and Milton, Wordsworth, Hardy and Larkin'.[5] The most commonly noticed verbal effect is in sonnet 4 (which I think is as important as 2 and 3), in which the poet and his mother agree on a 'middle voice' to avoid the difficulties of pretension or condescension:

> She'd manage something hampered and askew
> Every time, as if she might betray
> The hampered and inadequate by too
> Well-adjusted a vocabulary.
> With more challenge than pride, she'd tell me, 'You
> Know all them things.'

(HL 28)

The calculated grammatical 'error' is well considered both by the mother and by the reporting poet. The calculation involved is underlined by what follows, as if Heaney is ensuring that his register is not misread again:

> So I governed my tongue
> In front of her, a genuinely well-
> adjusted adequate betrayal
> Of what I knew better. I'd *naw* and *aye*
> And decently relapse into the wrong
> Grammar which kept us allied and at bay.
>
> (*HL* 28)

The connection between decency and technical error might make us review Joyce's adjuration in 'Station Island' against doing 'the decent thing'. It may be technically wrong, as it is here, and still be the right (because the decent) thing to do.

There are more missable linguistic misprisions elsewhere in these sonnets. A notably subtle one comes in sonnet 2 (rightly one of Allen's ageless anthology pieces; it does have more obvious local usages too: 'don't be dropping crumbs'). The more elusive misusage comes as the poet, remembering the domestic rules of childhood, intones:

> Sandwich and teascone
> Were present and correct. In case it run,
> The butter must be kept out of the sun.
>
> (*HL* 26)

What is the grammatical status of 'run' in the second line? It would be a correct use of the present subjunctive for the conditional – 'lest it run' – (as Heaney well knows); but that is unlikely to be the explanation of this form here. It is more probable that it is a classic grammatical solecism, common in several dialects of English (especially Irish ones) and a shibboleth popular with grammatical pedants since the eighteenth century: past participle for past tense. It should be 'In case it ran'. But the question then arises: in whose person is the solecism voiced? It is certainly not the mother's direct speech, nor the poet's own grammar. It is a perfect instance of the 'middle-voiced' grammar that keeps speakers 'allied and at bay'. An obvious comparison is, again, with Tony Harrison's 'Them and [*uz*]', but there is an important difference: Harrison sees linguistic difference as a dividing force which can be used as a weapon; Heaney sees its potential, as in all verbal effects, of positive application. Linguistic difference can achieve alliance as well as hostility.

113

Despite the importance of these poems as brilliant examples of the 'middle voice', these elegies seem – like Douglas Dunn's great volume *Elegies* in memory of his wife – to be special-occasion poems, not to be brought in evidence in assessing the progress of Heaney's aesthetic for the lyric poet. The Eastern European, parabling poems in *The Haw Lantern* are doing something very different, perhaps addressing the theory of artistic freedom more squarely than anything else in Heaney's poetry. His prose does address it constantly, as I shall argue in the next chapter; so does *The Cure at Troy*, his adaptation of Sophocles' *Philoctetes*.[7] As I said in the Introduction, there is little precedent in the English poetic tradition (before Yeats, at least) for discussion of art/life imperatives of the kind that Heaney needs to address after *Station Island*. Hence his need to borrow the underground form of the Eastern European lyric, which automatically evokes issues of artistic freedom.

These associations are brought to bear on Heaney's situation, both as Northern Irishman and as poet. We remember Heaney's status of 'inner émigré', claimed in 'Exposure' (a poem which comes to mind more than once in reading this volume). For example, 'From the Land of the Unspoken' begins like an anthropological case study:

> I have heard of a bar of platinum
> kept by a logical and talkative nation
> as their standard of measurement.
>
> (*HL* 18)

The word that seems out of place here, because it is too friendly, is 'talkative'; and it gradually dawns on the reader that the nation in question, and the 'we' who are in 'exile ... among the speech-ridden', fits the Heaney–Sweeney situation very well, bearing in mind the 'famous northern reticence' and the much-quoted advice: 'Whatever You Say Say Nothing'. But it fits equally well the pre-verbal, intuitive learner of 'Alphabets'.

These poems are most successful, because most in Heaney's best vein, when they move away from the ingenious-abstract towards the personal and emotional. His gift is for the graphic. So, in 'From the Land of the Unspoken', it is a relief to encounter this 'deepest contact' in the third stanza:

strap-hanging back to back on a rush-hour train
and in a museum once, I inhaled
vernal assent from a neck and shoulder.

(HL 18)

It is even more of a relief when the somewhat mannered opening
stanza of 'Grotus and Coventina' gets fed up with the mythopoeic
(Coventina 'holds in her right hand a waterweed/ And in her left a
pitcher spilling out a river') to be released into the reality of
memory:

Remember when our electric pump gave out,
Priming it with bucketfuls, our idiotic rage
And hangdog phone-calls to the farm next door
For somebody please to come and fix it?

(HL 40)

The self-mockery suggests that Heaney, too, finds the mythic
portentousness of what went before less to his taste.

After 'Alphabets', the poem in *The Haw Lantern* which
addresses the language theme most directly is one of the best of
these parable poems, 'From the Canton of Expectation'. As well as
imposing coherence by returning to the 'scale of being' of verbs,
the poem is a notable instance of how these poems at their best
mix autobiographical material with the more abstract parable
form. It begins with a metaphorical twist on the anthropological
description:

We lived deep in a land of optative moods,
under high, banked clouds of resignation.

(HL 46)

The 'optative mood' again plays on forms of the verb. In the
progress from the 'pure verb' aspiration of *Field Work*, past the
inactive participles of 'In Illo Tempore' in *Station Island*, an even
less active form of the verb has been reached, capable of nothing
more than the notional wish that action should take place. This
non-fulfilment is reinforced by the Northern Irish Catholic terms
of phatic communion, *Not in our lifetime* and 'the broken nerve'
betrayed by the cowed verbs of prayer '*Vouchsafe*' and '*Deign*'.[8]
(Heaney is fond of these community-building phatic terms: they

are found again, for example, in 'The Sounds of Rain', his elegy for Richard Ellmann: '*He'll be missed* and *You'll have to thole*', where it is striking that the formulaic Irish one is matched by one of Heaney's favourite Ulster-Englishisms, 'thole' (*ST* 48).)

These terms are useful in 'From the Canton of Expectation' in establishing that the Northern nationalist community is indeed the tribe in question. This is further confirmed by the description in the next paragraph of the Irish dancing festival, the *Feis*, in entirely literal, historical terms:

> When our rebel anthem played the meeting shut
> we turned for home and the usual harassment
> by militiamen on overtime at roadblocks.

However, the poem's second and third sections sustain the balance between memory, parable and linguistic metaphor. The change in historical circumstances, from resignation to civil rights agitation, is described half-punningly as a 'change of mood'. The optatives are replaced by 'a grammar of imperatives' which 'would banish the conditional for ever', though we notice the auxiliary 'would' in passing as insuperably optative still.

This unfulfilled condition is reaffirmed in section III of the poem, when 'the indicative' is – optatively – yearned for as something in the past or in the unforeseeable future. As one might expect from a poem on the Eastern European political model, the linguistic terminology here transcends its metaphorical nature to come close to paraphrasable political statement. Such a paraphrase might be something like this: the resigned placebos of the past, when second-class citizenship in Northern Ireland was taken as normal, have lost even the capacity to console after the 'new age of demands' for civil rights has proved unfulfilling. Once again, we encounter ineffectuality in language, this time to express political ineffectuality. The poem ends, as in 'Alphabets' and earlier Heaney, with a desperate wish for accuracy, clarity and indicative assertion, like 'hammerblows on clinkered planks,/ the uncompromised report of driven thole-pins' (*HL* 47).

This poem, especially its conclusion, should be read in conjunction with some of the essays in *The Government of the Tongue*, especially 'The Impact of Translation' (*GT* 36–44) and the final essay, on Sylvia Plath (148–70). For example, the word 'report' in the lines just quoted, with its double sense of 'sound' and 'verbal message', makes the same phonetic link as does this sentence from the Plath essay: 'We are reminded how *persona* derives from *personare*, meaning "to sound out through", how the animation of verb lives in the mask's noun-like impassiveness' (*GT* 149).

In a further, equally crucial parallel, Heaney writes of 'the implacably indicative mood' of Plath's harrowing poem 'Edge'. The application of the term 'indicative' to Plath suggests that it means something more general than the wish for decisiveness in *political* expression (though it means that too) which Alan Robinson interprets it as in his excellent discussion of Heaney.[9] The major discussion of 'the indicative' by Heaney himself, which supports Robinson's reading, comes in the vital section of 'The Impact of Translation', where he is discussing the intimate relation between phonetics and feeling 'in the human make-up' (*GT* 39). Writing of the 'heroic names' who have stood up for artistic values against totalitarian conformism in twentieth-century Russian literature, Heaney writes, with uncharacteristic acerbity:

> For these poets, the mood of writing is the indicative mood and for that reason they constitute a shadow-challenge to poets who dwell in the conditional, the indeterminate mood which has grown characteristic of so much of the poetry one has grown used to reading in the journals and new books, particularly in the United States. (*GT* 39)

This is recognisably another expression of the ideal of writing transparently, transferred from the phonetic and lexical to the grammatical. It is important to see that grammatical metaphors need not be 'dry', in a poem like 'From the Canton of Expectation'; to draw on Yeats's formula again, syntax can be passionate. That, too, is linked to feeling, as it is in the Russian poets and Plath. Something of Plath's desperation is carried into the poem, where (as in Plath) the choice seems to be between the unfulfilled optative and the indicative statement which requires the finality of death before it can be used with certainty. This is further suggested by the noun's 'impassiveness', which in Heaney is a logical further stage again down the verb's scale of being: on the descent from activeness beyond passiveness to a totally static condition.

The Haw Lantern is such a various collection that it is impossible to generalise about its metrical forms. It does return to rhyme, which had been almost totally absent from *Station Island*, in a number of poems. One of these, 'A Peacock's Feather', is an occasional poem dating from 1972. Just as 'Antaeus' was formally anachronistic in *North* (N 12), so this poem, for all its charm, is full of effects that have been left behind, as if to remind us how much Heaney's poetic has moved on. There are the *deibidhe* rhymes ('brick/nostalgic'; 'lay/Bradley'; 'intimacy/say'), as well as a rather self-conscious, urbane accomplishment which is no longer Heaney's serious manner. 'A Daylight Art', which is universally seen as one of the book's principal successes outside the 'Clearances' sequence, illustrates well the effective mix of formality and vernacular freedom which is such a recurrent feature of *Seeing Things*, and gives the desired impression of frank accuracy. The way conversational fillers like 'now' or 'say' are used is a clear example:

> Caesar, now, or Herod or Constantine . . .
>
> you can believe in their believing dreams . . .
>
> Happy the man, therefore, with a natural gift
>
> for practising the right one from the start –
> poetry, say, or fishing.
>
> (HL 9)

This achieves a middle register between a high style's 'alluding' (this eloquent poem, after all, 'alludes' to Shakespeare just as clearly as the mocked lecturer of 'Alphabets') and the colloquial language which has been the definitive element in many modern Irish poets, such as Durcan or Kennelly. Heaney is travelling yet another middle course: between their freestyle poetic and the classicism (which can seem unbending) of his most distinguished Northern contemporaries, Mahon and Longley.

Despite the linguistic determinacy of its starting point, 'Alphabets', *The Haw Lantern* retains an open-endedness, appropriate to its sceptical view of language. Hart wants to see it as having a sustained deconstructive view of language. We know, it is true, from *The Government of the Tongue*, that Heaney is familiar with the insights of deconstruction (Hart 179), but that hardly warrants regarding the beautiful 'A Daylight Art' as a poem which 'deconstructs Socrates'. Heaney's fondness for deconstructive etymological runs in *The Government of the Tongue* amounts to no more, I think, than an inquisitiveness about the inner workings of particular words: geological rather than philosophical. Not only does *The Haw Lantern* end with the least conclusive closing poem of any Heaney volume, aptly as 'The Riddle' represents the dilemma of the content of art; it strikingly *does not* end with its epic fragment, 'A Ship of Death', which is an admirable plainstyle translation of Scyld's funeral from *Beowulf*.[10] To have ended with that, as *Field Work* ended with Dante's 'Ugolino' and *Seeing Things* will end with Charon from *Inferno*, would have suggested a conclusiveness which is not appropriate to the consideration of whether poetry 'makes anything happen' – which is, broadly, the theme of this book, just as it is of the similarly Eastern European-inspired contemporary prose deliberations in *The Government of the Tongue*. The next book will return to more personal issues, accordingly treating language and its metaphorical possibilities in very different ways.

Seeing Things

> Me waiting until I was nearly fifty
> To credit marvels. ('Fosterling')

The remarkable claim made in Heaney's most recent book is that the movement away from the material opacity of the language of the early poetry towards a more transparent medium is complete. This, of course, is no more than an aesthetic idea; but the theme of transparency is very insistent in the book, highlighted by its place in the title-poem, especially in the second section's stress on the 'utter visibility' of the *Claritas* of the 'unshadowed stream' (*ST* 17).

This thematic clarity, which the linguistic transparency serves, is crucial to the book's central concern. One of the most important mediating functions of the poet throughout Heaney's career has been as diviner or *vates*, from the early well-poems such as

'Personal Helicon' onwards. In those poems the mediation was between personal consciousness, and knowledge of history and the world. But Heaney became increasingly insistent that this divination, like the ideal of translation, must be as little obscured by its medium as possible. *Seeing Things* sets itself an extremely ambitious programme of mediations: between this world and the next, between youth and age, between the terrestrial and the extra-terrestrial. Because it is so concerned with crossing over between these realms, with various *rites de passage*, the volume is full of thresholds. The linguistic implications are obvious: some contemporary literary theorists see the essence of language as its 'liminality',[11] its function as mediator.

The theme of *The Haw Lantern* varied from section to section, from the elegiac to the political. *Seeing Things* remains intent on thresholds and crossings throughout its formally very different parts. Like many of the earlier volumes, it is organised into distinct blocks, but here more markedly so than ever before: more so even than *Station Island*. Part I consists of a series of lyrics of various lengths and subjects; Part II is a group of forty-eight twelve-line poems of a kind which first appeared in *Station Island*, apparently as by-products of the *terza rima* of the central sequence but now, for the most part, refined into a tighter form, more traditional in the English lyric. Heaney's fondness for anglicised *terza rima* goes back as far as the 'Lough Neagh Sequence' in *Door into the Dark*. In *Seeing Things* a more marked formal tightness is balanced by a looseness of vocabulary, often drawing on local usage. The hostage given to critical fortune, laying him open to the charge of inexpertise, in Heaney's earlier work was in the field of metrics; now it is in lexis and syntax.

These forty-eight poems are divided into four groups of twelve, all appearing under the general heading 'Squarings', which is also the title of the fourth group. However, the impression of dominance that this repetition of title might make is undercut by the fact that Heaney tells us (in the Bragg interview, for example) he had considered using the name of the first group, 'Lightenings', for the whole volume. For that matter, the title of the third group, 'Crossings', is also the title given to the translation from Canto III of *Inferno* which comes at the end, balancing a translation, 'The Golden Bough', from *Aeneid* VI which starts the book. These two fifty-line blocks stand outside the structure of the book, so on those grounds the term 'Crossings' might be thought more authoritative than the repeated 'Squarings'.

This sounds terminological, but the point is essential to the theme of *Seeing Things*. There is no doubt, I think, that this is one of Heaney's high-profile books, in the tradition from *Death of a Naturalist*, to *Wintering Out/North*, to *Station Island*. 'Crossings' – the mediation between the underworld and our world, as well as that between our world and the afterlife – would have been an appropriate title for the volume. I suspect that it was ruled out by its eschatological grandness.

But it is crucial to see the centrality of this idea in the book. Language, of course, is the most universal crossing of all, because transference of meaning – 'translation' – is its very nature. A poem early in the book, 'Markings', could be read as an exposition of this metaphor. Indeed, it is hard not to read it, once the linguistic parallel has been introduced, in Saussurean terms, as an expression of the essential arbitrariness of the linguistic sign. For this reason, it is hard to agree with the later stages in Hart's book, where he argues that the binary oppositions he quotes from Heaney are 'deconstructing' the logocentric tradition from Socrates to Saussure. 'Markings' might have been written (though I am sure it wasn't) as an allegory of Saussure's view of the efficiency of arbitrary language structure.[12]

The poem begins very fetchingly with the marking out by children of a pitch for Gaelic Football:

> We marked the pitch: four jackets for four goalposts,
> That was all. The corners and the squares
> Were there like longitude and latitude
> Under the bumpy, thistly ground.
>
> (*ST* 8)

This idea – that the pitch markings are present *under* the ground, though not visible on it – is developed in the contexts of *rites de passage*:

> their own hard
> Breathing in the dark and skids on grass
> Sounded like effort in another world . . .
> Some limit had been passed.
> (*ibid.*)

Beneath the football pitch some underworld (probably, in this context, the Elysian Fields) is marked out, bearing a validating relation to our world.

The poem's second section takes another pleasing set of markings, those used in handiwork: the string used by gardeners to mark rows, or by builders in starting a house, or the *imaginary* (again) line used by the farmer to plough a straight furrow from one end of a field to the other. This links obviously to the notional lines within which the boys played football; what both things share with language is the quality of being taken for granted. The rules of language, like these notional pitch markings, are not demonstrable entities, but the activities they delimit cannot take place without their being grasped, however imperfectly, 'to be/ Agreed about or disagreed about/ When the time came'.

This is remarkably close to the idea of language as inconclusive (but essential) which Heaney has been developing. There are other slight supporting clues in the poem: for example, the grass on which the house-builder lays 'each freshly sawn new board/ Spick and span' is described as 'oddly passive'. By a kind of linguistic transference, the adverb applies more to the odd application of the grammatical term 'passive' to the grass than it does to the word 'passive' itself.

If the linguistic comparison sounds far-fetched, its applicability is confirmed by the poem's strange but compelling third section. This begins with an idea that recalls again the discussion of priority at the end of Yeats's 'Among School Children':[13] 'All these things entered you/ As if they were both the door and what came through it (*ST* 9).

In this way, language is both medium and expression; it is hard to see what else this second line fits. And the poem ends with a wonderful image of co-operation and communication:

> Two men with a cross-cut kept it swimming
> Into a felled beech backwards and forwards
> So that they seemed to row the steady earth.
> (*ST* 9)

This beautiful image (as well as recalling the cover illustration of *Station Island*, taken from the medieval manuscript of Giraldus's *History and Topography of Ireland*[14]) links well with other parts of *Seeing Things* in which, in a traditional figure, crossing water is the most favoured image of threshold.

The underlying linguistic theory in this book is less explicitly addressed than in many of its predecessors. There is nothing corresponding to the way in which, for example, the 'phonetic fiction' is spelt out in *Wintering Out*, but it is at least as important as it is in any of the other books. One of the several operative senses of the title-phrase, 'seeing things', is the imagining of what is not literally there. This obviously applies to the pitch markings on the football field, or the straight line along which the ploughman takes his bearings; but it also recalls the idea of absence which was prominent earlier, particularly in *North*. Combining this with another sense of 'seeing things' – the mystic's vision – we are struck by the pervasiveness of statement by denial (the rhetorical figure *oppositum*) here: the 'unsayability' *topos*.

Before proceeding to more classical instances of this, we might note one that recalls the *gh* phoneme of 'Broagh', in this line from 'A Retrospect': 'With Chichester in 1608' (*ST* 42). How is the date to be pronounced? The hendecasyllabic model of the line before might suggest 'sixteen-hundred-and-eight', given a slightly ungainly line; 'sixteen-o-eight' is a syllable short, but that is hardly conclusive. The line functions as another failure in language: this time a failure to work back from the written form to the spoken.

Negativing prefixes are common throughout the book. The most memorable is the adjective in the first line of the third section of the title-poem, in the phrase 'my undrowned father' (18). It serves its purpose perfectly: the point being made is that the father was not drowned when his drowning was likely (like Tom Brangwen in Lawrence's *The Rainbow*,[15] which this section evokes – I think not accidentally). But the parallel of 'undead' is disturbing, for several reasons: first, its inherent ghoulishness; second, because the father now *is* dead, as we know well, since the book has several unlaboured and graceful elegies for him; third, because the word, like the apparition, is oddly suspended between life and death, maybe recalling the schoolgoer's riddle 'would you rather be nearly drowned or nearly saved?'. This liminal condition is recurrent in the book, mostly through the use of the favourite Dante-translating noun 'shade' (rather than 'the dawn-sniffing revenant' of *Station Island*); for example, in unlikely application to Larkin in the first poem of Part I. The liminal condition of the father in this book of thresholds is unmistakeable in the Christ-reference towards the end of the poem:

> That afternoon
> I saw him face to face, he came to me
> With his damp footprints out of the river.
>
> (*ST* 18)

Word-formations similar to 'undrowned' occur in the sixth sonnet in the 'Glanmore Revisited' sequence, 'Bedtime Reading', where the figure is used eloquently to evade facing up to grief. The lovers' secret at the end is 'unsaid', balancing the negatives at the end of the octet with the Audenesque adjective 'unfurtive': 'With wet, unreadable, unfurtive eyes' (*ST* 36). Again, language is operating according to its structural rules, but failing: the adjective should be contradictable by the *un-* prefix; but if its meaning is already negative, it becomes ambiguous. Does it mean the positive opposite of furtive: 'transparent' or merely 'not furtive'? Does Auden's 'unhated' mean 'loved'?[16] It would according to the rules of rhetoric, and it would in Latin and in Milton; but it does not seem to now. Something similar occurs in 'A Retrospect', though this time less ambiguously in its context:

> No nest in rushes, the heather bells unbruised,
> The love-drink of the mountain streams untasted.
>
> (*ST* 43)

(This poem offers another interesting opportunity to compare the styles of different periods, like 'Antaeus' and 'A Peacock's Feather', since the waterlogged opening section appeared as 'Mayday' in *The New Statesman* twenty years earlier. The vibrant descriptive language of that part – 'the swim and flow/ From hidden springs made a river in the road' (*ST* 42) – contrasts strikingly with the kind of hedged-in linguistic devices I am considering here.)

The culminating instance of negativing forms comes in a highly evocative poem in the 'Crossings' series:

> Not an avenue and not a bower . . .
>
> You drive into a meaning made of trees.
> Or not exactly trees.
>
> (xxxi: *ST* 89)

The linguistic importance of this haunting poem (about driving through an avenue of Scotch firs) comes in the phrase 'a meaning made of trees'. We remember the lungs and uvulae of objects: the language that is more expressive through observation, even if it does not reach verbal form.

But the most important thing this line establishes is that these uses of *oppositum*, like the mystical *via negativa* and 'Dark Night of the Soul', are entirely positive in their meaning. If Hart had reached *Seeing Things*, he would have found that his mystical model from *Door into the Dark* yields dividends there. We should remember what Heaney said in the 'South Bank Show' interview about the difference between *Station Island* and *Seeing Things*: in *Station Island* the 'sweetness of lyric is refused', and the book 'tries to put the boot into lyric'. Its concentration on the 'music of what happens' was put in remarkably negative terms in that interview, to mean an undesired confinement to public realities. *Seeing Things* is a return to desire: to 'the music of what might happen'. One of the ironies of Desmond Fennell's attack on Heaney is that it accuses him of being too attentive to 'the clankings, hisses, whistling, thuds and gratings' of 'the music of what happens' to be melodious.[17] Heaney says something similar to this in the Bragg interview: that he now wants to hear the more poetic music of what *might* happen. But Fennell's objection here is in direct conflict with his main demand – that Heaney should be more politically assertive: that is, more attentive to the everyday, public 'music of what happens', as *Station Island* was.

Thus the deficiencies of language's expressive power are not, in the end, to be seen as negative at all. No reader could fail to notice that *Seeing Things*, whatever its lexical structures, is a decidedly positive book. This is stated most luminously in its most pro-grammatic poem, 'Fosterling', which uses a wide range of linguistic registers to make its case. Most of Heaney's linguistic stages are represented here: the materialist aesthetic and heavy diction of *Death of a Naturalist*, with what is now called its 'Heaviness of being'; *Wintering Out*'s many-stranded colloquial-ism of Ulster usage, with its dialectal English and Scottish components: 'Of *glar* and *glit* and floods at *dailigone*' (*ST* 50). All this is conceded as once 'loved', but now characterised as 'poetry/ Sluggish in the doldrums of what happens' (*ST* 50).

The striking point here is that Heaney is simply redefining the 'music of what happens', whether it is in *Station Island* or elsewhere, as 'the doldrums'. For all the beauty of Finn's answer to the question 'What is the best music?', 'what happens', it is now suggested, is not the best music for poetry. There is further play with this formula in *Seeing Things*. For example, poem v in the 'Lightenings' sequence returns to the elusive 'half-said thing' in a variation on the phrase which seems to me to come down decisively on the side of the responsible against the ludic: this is an adjuration, along the lines of *Station Island*'s Joyce, to 'Improvise. Make free/ Like old hay in its flimsy afterlife// High on a windblown hedge' (*ST* 59). Surely this cannot be poetry's highest calling either: a reservation which is confirmed by the particular variation of Finn's formula, 'the music of the arbitrary'.

Despite the limitations of 'what happens' as the tune for poetry, Heaney does stick with a version of description as revelation in this book. The ambitious project of *Seeing Things*, from 'Fosterling', has already been quoted often: 'Me waiting until I was nearly fifty/ To credit marvels' (*ST* 50). After the rigours of *Station Island*, it is 'Time to be dazzled and the heart to lighten' (*ST* 50). But the marvels, curiously, are such things as 'the tree-clock of tin cans/ The tinkers made'; we recall Michael Allen's protest against the Joyce advice to 'fill the element/ with signatures on your own frequency' (*SI* 94). Allen comments that this 'is what he had actually *started off* doing anyway'.[18] Well before *Seeing Things* there are many emblematic marvels of the same kind as the tinkers' tree-clocks.

But Heaney has stressed the importance of this image by calling his interim book published by The Linen Hall Library in Belfast *The Tree Clock* (1990).[19] There 'Fosterling' comes as the conclusion (and the *Inferno* translation 'The Crossing' is in the middle of the book). The tree-clock's significance, I think, is as a kind of graven image from the secular mysticism which is this book's religion and the principal operative sense of 'seeing things'. This quasi-religion is evident in the way traditional religious terminology is applied in secular contexts, investing them with a strong sense of occasion. One example of this secular application of hieratic language is in 'Settings' xxi, when the white handkerchief which the fired gun snatches away is compared (in a Yeatsian symbol) to the soul 'as it was in the beginning' (*ST* 77).

Two further examples come in the title-poem: Part III (about the 'undrowned' father) refers to 'his ghosthood immanent'. Ghosthood in this sense is always 'immanent' in everybody, because we are mortal; but the term is usually reserved for the transcendent and immortal. The second example is more important, because it is central to the whole book's meaning. Part I of 'Seeing Things' ends with these visionary humanist lines:

> It was as if I looked from another boat
> Sailing through air, far up, and could see
> How riskily we fared into the morning,
> And loved in vain our bare, bowed, numbered heads.
>
> (ST 16)

The most striking word in that tellingly slowed last line is 'numbered'. This biblical verb is encountered in the liturgy as an indication of the materialist frailty of the physical body, most familiar in the verses of the Psalms: 'They have pierced my hands and feet; they have numbered all my bones'.[20]

The perspective in these lines – of a ship in the air looking down on our reality – occurs again in a poem which is as assured as anything Heaney has written, 'Lightenings' viii. I am quoting it in full, because I believe it is an outstanding example of Heaney's matured style:

> The annals say: when the monks of Clonmacnoise
> Were all at prayers inside the oratory
> A ship appeared above them in the air.
>
> The anchor dragged along behind so deep
> It hooked itself into the altar rails
> And then, as the big ship rocked to a standstill,
>
> A crewman shinned and grappled down the rope
> And struggled to release it. But in vain.
> 'This man can't bear our life here and will drown,'
>
> The abbot said, 'unless we help him.' So
> They did, the freed ship sailed, and the man climbed back
> Out of the marvellous as he had known it.
>
> (ST 62)

The last line is the crucial one: the marvellous is what is seen to be marvellous. The normal world is as remarkable from the viewpoint of a ship that sails in the air as that ship is to us. Underlying the poem, too, is the notion of 'in its element': the idea of the fish out of water that 'drowns' in air, as we do in water.

The dialectal implications of the moving between elements are also richly exploited by Heaney. From the opening Virgil translation ('He was praying *like that*') to the closing Dante ('They go away *like this*') the poet reserves the right to draw on informal usage, taken from colloquial registers (emphases added). In the last of the 'Lightenings' poems, the definition of this term for secular mysticism (a term which might have been the whole book's title, and provides a good deal of its meaning) is given with great insouciance:

> And lightening? One meaning of that
> Beyond the usual sense of alleviation,
> Illumination, and so on, is this . . .
> (*ST* 66)

There are occasions where the reapplication of colloquialisms and clichés borders on the reckless:

> It seemed to be all rise
> and shine, the very opposite
>
> of uphill going.
> ('The Pulse': *ST* 11)

The function of this colloquial insistence is clear enough. The secular mysticism of the book is a celebration of the ordinary, sometimes in its transcendent form, and ordinary language can be drawn on in representing it. Heaney's dead father is the book's tutelary spirit, and these lines from 'Man and Boy' are the poem's centre:

> Blessed be down-to-earth! Blessed be highs!
> Blessed be the detachment of dumb love
> In that broad-backed, low-set man
> Who feared debt all his life, but now and then
> Could make a splash like the salmon he said was
> 'As big as a wee pork pig by the sound of it'.
> (*ST* 14)

The ordinary and its expression, or lack of it – its 'dumb love' is the famous Northern reticence – is exalted here. The colloquialism 'make a splash' echoes throughout this book, but it means 'is exalted' too. Finally, 'by the sound of it' recalls the whole 'phonetic fantasy': the inextricability of sound and meaning which has been the basis of Heaney's poetic from the first.

I have been arguing throughout this book that Heaney is a highly considered poet: that his – to quote the last line of the first poem, 'Squarings' – is 'an art that knows its mind' (*ST* 97). The poet's 'middle voice', which has to negotiate with several languages and views of the world, takes its stand at different points according to the requirements of its particular subject. The bias of *Seeing Things* towards the blessed 'down-to-earth' generates a mixed language, with its bias towards the vernacular end of the spectrum. In addition to the instances of this given already, we might note the Ulster dialect usages: 'rusted' in 'Seeing Things' for a horse shying;[21] and *glar, glit* and *dailigone* in 'Fosterling', noted above. It may be necessary (alas!) to provide the information that 'The Point' in 'Three Drawings' (*ST* 10) is the score recorded in Gaelic Football when the ball is kicked over the crossbar. On the other hand, there are English high-style archaisms: 'handsel' (*ST* 30) and 'cantreds' (*ST* 43). The first of these occurs in 'The Schoolbag', Heaney's elegy for the Ulster poet John Hewitt, which – entirely appropriately for its subject – extends across a wide lexical range, from the traditional English 'handsel' and 'word-hoard' to the Norse-derived 'trig' (dialectal for 'trim, spruce') and the Ulster colloquial '*Learning's easy carried*!'.

What is most striking and novel in this volume is a series of Irish syntactic usages which are striking only after mature deliberation, like the 'run' butter in 'Clearances'. Take these lines from 'A Haul':

> The hole he smashed in the boat
> opened, the way Thor's head
> opened out there on the sea.
> (*ST* 12)

'The way' might be read as the Irishism for 'so that', 'with the result that' (from the Irish *gur*). A similarly equivocal example is the first line of the elegy for Heaney's father, 'The Ash Plant': 'He'll never rise again but he is ready' (*ST* 19). In addition to its normal English sense, this 'but' may carry the Irish sense 'without being'. Such usages are punned on at the opening of 'The Settle

Bed', which is 'in place at last and for good': the primary meaning of the colloquial last two words 'for ever' (with the additional sense of 'to salutary effect'). The title of one of Heaney's notable post-*Seeing Things* poems, 'Poet's Chair', draws on it for its culminating line: 'Of being here for good in every sense'.[22]

It must be stressed that the language of *Seeing Things* is an 'ordinary' English language too. Indeed, it probably makes less dialectal demand on the Standard English reader than *Death of a Naturalist* did, unnoticed. Some of the graphic linguistic effects exploit recent developments in Standard English too. For example, Heaney's progressively reduced activeness in verbs is facilitated by the tendency in English (ever since Old English, but steadily accelerating since the sixteenth century) to form verbs from nouns by simple conversion without inflection: the process called 'zero derivation'. The passage from 'The Pulse' I have already quoted – 'all rise/ and shine' – contains two; the poem goes on to describe 'all of that/ runaway *give*', and ends with 'the river's/ steady /*purchase* and *thrum*' (11; emphases added). In 'Settings' xvi he says: 'I loved its *reek* and *risk*' (72; emphasis added). They are too standard in modern English to take much note of; but they serve Heaney's objective very well in converting the will towards 'pure verb' to stasis. The mixed diction and register that have been such a calculated risk throughout Heaney's writing occur here in another exploited feature of modern English which has been much favoured by such romantic poets as Hopkins, Dylan Thomas and Heaney's often-cited Irish poet Francis Ledwidge: what Barbara Strang, in *A History of English*, calls 'compound lexical items'.[23] This is the grammatical tendency which treats phrases as single words, in poetry usually adjectives: Hopkins's 'dapple-dawn-drawn falcon'; Thomas's 'heron-priested shore'; Ledwidge's 'spider-peopled wells'. Heaney introduces variations on these compounds, in the title-poem's 'seeable-down-into water' (16); in 'un-get-round-able weight' in 'The Settle Bed' (28); in the noun 'up-againstness' ('Lightenings' x, 64); and in 'the end-of-summer, stone-walled fields' ('Squarings' xlvi, 106). These formations link with the figure of 'unsayability': now the language's syntax, as previously its vocabulary, lacks the resources to express what is required.

Because the language itself rather than the metalinguistic commentary is central in *Seeing Things*, the philological metaphors are not so prominent. But Heaney's concern with language – here more urgently with language as medium – means that the terms of linguistic analysis are still common. The elegy for the archaeologist Tom Delaney uses the most inevitable one in the context of this book of thresholds: the memorial scrabbling of the pen is 'intransitive', both formally and by implication, because it does not cross over to the afterlife. 'Untranslatable' occurs with a similar force in 'Lightenings' xii, the definitions poem. There is one place where the logical precedence that language took over event in earlier Heaney (as in 'The Birthplace') is reasserted again, at the end of the poem of mystical stillness, 'Settings' xxiv:

> Air and ocean known as antecedents
> Of each other. In apposition with
> Omnipresence, equilibrium, brim.
> (*ST* 80)

The equivalence and reference between word and object can be described as appositional in this way: as apposite, as well as performing the same grammatical function.

It might be noted in a preliminary way that Heaney's post-*Seeing Things* poems seem to be using grammatical terminology very prominently. In an important programmatic poem, 'Here for Good',[24] the imagistic reference to the suckling of Romulus and Remus is interrupted to give a short dictionary gloss on the Latin word *uber*: '(Third declension, neuter, *breast* or *bosom*)'. There is an interesting inversion of use and mention here: the English words which are the poem's topic are italicised: the grammatical gloss is not, as if that were the real language of the poem. The conflicting use of Jakobsonian ordinary, poetic and glossing languages may be related to the poem's decidedly modernist look on the page: it is in five sections, of various lengths and styles, like Yeats's 'Nineteen Hundred and Nineteen'.

There are lesser linguistic metaphors throughout *Seeing Things*, because these are now so much a part of Heaney's metaphorical language: words like 'plosive', 'singular', 'declension' and 'tenses', for example. But the last group of metalinguistic terms to be considered is both the most predictable one in this context of linguistic mediacy, and the most important for the book's meaning. They might be called – adapting the terms of Austin's

Pragmatics – speech acts in writing.[25] The word '*Stet!*' comes at the end of 'Wheels within Wheels', again punning on the orthographic instruction that what has been written should stand because it is accurate, and the declared wish that the circus-ring images of childhood should remain. More strikingly again, there are two instances of the term hieroglyph, as a form of writing that overcomes Saussurean arbitrariness through graphic rather than calligraphic representation: at the end of 'Seeing Things' – 'Like the zig-zag hieroglyph for life itself' (*ST* 17) – and in the curious hare-poem which refers to the same figure in a very striking piece of footnoting metalanguage:

> the ancient hieroglyph
> Of 'hare and zig-zag', which meant 'to exist'.
> ('Squarings' xliii: *ST* 103)

Finally, these linguistic representations, which are not alienated from reality by abstractions, lead into a brief repetition of the point that the metrical forms in *Seeing Things* have ostensible aspirations towards the accuracy of direct utterance in the tradition of English lyric, by contrast with the materialist obstructions of the language in *Death of a Naturalist* and *Wintering Out*. Parochial vivifying is provided here through syntax and vocabulary, as I have shown; the metrical form is almost invariably the English two-syllable iambic (or its inverted form, the trochaic, which can be seen as a headless iambic in the pentameter). Anywhere in the twelve-line poems shows this:

> A boat that did not rock or wobble once
> (63)

> The annals say: when the monks of Clonmacnoise
> (62)

The second example here illustrates an advantage of a regular 'home' metre (beyond the transparency of its reassuring familiarity): it is what Yeats calls, in 'A General Introduction for My Work', a 'ghostly voice',[26] there to be varied upon for musical effect. The Clonmacnoise line has a rapid extra non-stress in the middle, giving a transient anapestic variation. Heaney is an expert,

as we know from the *deibidhe* era of 'Follower': as a final
example, we might take the Chaucerian trochaic inversion of
'contents' and 'order' here: 'Its own contents in meaningful order'
(*ST* 75). I have already noted Heaney's fondness for the Yeatsian
list of trochees ('horseback, assback, muleback'), as in these long
lines in *Seeing Things*:

> Sunlight, turfsmoke, seagulls, boatslip, diesel.
> (16)

> Smoothness, straightness, roundness, length and sheen.
> (23)

> And pew-strait, bin-deep, standing four-square as an ark.
> (28)

What is the function of this regularity? It can be linked to another
image which is second only to liminality in its pervasiveness in
Seeing Things: the idea of steadying as a 'guarantee' in the face of
transience which is the keynote of the prominent elegiacs of this
book. I have quoted already the great statement of impermanence
from 'Iron Spike' in *Station Island*. The title-poem here returns to
this idea, and refines it by observing that the very thing that
'guarantees us' – the boat's capacity to shift and adjust – is what
makes for the greatest sense of danger. In another poem of
unstable register (recalling Miss Walls in 'Death of a Naturalist')
the poet reminds himself of the child's learning the local dialect:
'A kesh could mean the track some called a *causey*' (90; emphasis
added), commenting rather enigmatically: 'It steadies me to tell
these things'. The culminating occurrence is in the Dantesque last
poem of 'Settings', xxxvi, describing the panicky return at the end
of a civil rights march to the car:

> Parked as we'd left it, that gave when we got in
> Like Charon's boat under the faring poets.
> (94)

This refers both backwards and forwards: back to 'Seeing Things',
from which we learned that it was the boat's yielding that saved
its passengers (an image, too, of political compromise); and
forwards to the translation of Dante's Charon in the epilogue
translation.

Steadiness and reassurance are needed – not only because of the sense of transience which is the unlaboured backdrop to the book in the figure of the poet's dead father, but because of the increasing uncertainty about language's ability to represent materially and unequivocally. In the final chapter I look at Heaney's extended discussion of this dilemma in *The Government of the Tongue*, which is primarily concerned, too, with the capacity of lyric language to express public responsibility. I take Dante in conjunction with this, because Heaney's Dante is the local-epic poet who marries perfect lyric form with political responsibility. In this way he is the answer to the different problems raised in both of Heaney's most recent books.

Heaney's *ars poetica*

Mandelstam, Dante and The Government of the Tongue

Between the two volumes considered in Chapter 4 came *The Government of the Tongue*, Heaney's fullest statement of his view of the freedoms and duties of the poet. What I want to do in this final chapter is to see how far this more abstracted theory of poetic language relates to the linguistic notions I have been tracing through the poems themselves.

It has been generally agreed that the distinction of Heaney's criticism is that it is unmistakeably the work of a practitioner, thereby satisfying the demands of modernists since Eliot that the critic of poetry should, ideally, also be a poet. It has been less often noted how total is Heaney's concentration on lyric poetry for his subject. The only essay in either of his collections of criticism, *Preoccupations* or *The Government of the Tongue*, which is not undistractably concerned with lyric poetry is a reprinted short and sharp *Times Literary Supplement* review of Brian Friel's play *Volunteers*, in which Heaney takes issue with the commentators on the play who had wished for a plainer political statement (P 214–16). Even there Heaney's touchstones are the exemplary lyric poets, Yeats ('out of the quarrel with ourselves we make poetry') and Wordsworth ('to create . . . the taste by which he is to be enjoyed': P 216).

In the Foreword to *Preoccupations* in 1980, Heaney declared clearly 'the central preoccupying questions' which have always been his critical subject: 'how should a poet properly live and write? What is his relationship to be to his own voice, his own place, his literary heritage and his contemporary world?' (*P* 13). There is an even more pronounced concentration on these preoccupying questions in his later critical collection *The Government of the Tongue* (1988) which, as was noted from the first reviews, 'is less miscellaneous than it appears'.[1] This time the declaration of intent is couched in rather more sophisticated terms, but it is essentially the same thing:

> what I had in mind was this aspect of poetry as its own vindicating force. In this dispensation, the tongue (representing both a poet's personal gift of utterance and the common resources of language itself) has been granted the right to govern. The poetic art is credited with an authority of its own. As readers we submit to the jurisdiction of achieved form...
>
> (*GT* 92)

Heaney's terminology claiming poetry's power to legislate is insistent here (recalling, of course, 'the unacknowledged legislators of the world' at the end of Shelley's *Defence of Poetry*): 'dispensation', 'the right to govern', 'authority', 'jurisdiction'. To see how the book's argument for this jurisdiction develops, the circumstances of its production must be briefly described. 'The Government of the Tongue' was the general title of Heaney's four 'T.S. Eliot Memorial Lectures', given at Eliot College, the University of Kent, in October 1986; and also the title of the first of them. The book of the same name, published in 1988, is divided into two parts: Part II is the Eliot Lectures, Part I is a series of eight previously published essays on various topics, all dealing with lyric poetry, particularly its language. Prefaced to the whole is a rewritten version of a paper that had already been published in two forms, the first as early as 1978.[2] Because of its debates about politics and the autonomy of poetry, some of its best reviewers read it enlighteningly in relation to the general political poems in *The Haw Lantern*, with titles on the model of 'From the x of y'. In Chapter 4 I discussed 'From the Canton of Expectation' in this connection, with its concluding yearning to stand one's 'ground in the indicative'.[3]

Of all the great poets, Dante is the one who most claims for poetry transcendent authority in personal and public matters. He has also been a major presence in Heaney's poetic practice since the Ugolino translation at the end of *Field Work*; he was most prominently drawn on in the penitential encounters in the 'Station Island' sequence, but there are other marks of his influence that are hardly less important: for example, the recurrence of *terza rima* from *The Haw Lantern* onwards, especially in the twelve-line 'Squarings' poems, and in the common appearances of the dead 'shades' (the favourite word since H.F. Cary in 1805 to translate Dante's *ombre*) throughout *Seeing Things*. One might, therefore, have expected him to have a central place in *The Government of the Tongue* among the poets: Kavanagh, Larkin, Walcott, Auden, Lowell, Plath and Bishop, as well as the East Europeans – Mandelstam, Milosz, Holub and Herbert – and the dispossessed classical Irish *filí*.

1. Mandelstam's Dante

Up to a point Dante does have this centrality in *The Government of the Tongue*, but indirectly, through a modern poet who *is* central in the book: Mandelstam. The organisation of *The Government of the Tongue* gives Mandelstam literal as well as metaphorical centrality. Part I ends with a reprint of Heaney's *London Review of Books* review of a package of Mandelstam items (listed *GT* 71), so that it immediately precedes the title-essay at the start of Part II, the Eliot Lectures, in which Mandelstam's 'astonishing fantasia on poetic creation, entitled . . . "A Conversation about Dante"' (*GT* 94)[4] is celebrated as 'a work of disconcertingly abundant genius, the greatest paean I know to the power which poetic imagination wields' (*GT* 95).

Not that we need an ulterior figure like Dante to justify Mandelstam's aptness to Heaney's view of poetry: Mandelstam is himself the classic 'inner émigré' whose poetry cannot be considered without reference to his political circumstances. It is the same attraction as a writer such as Milosz has, enabling Heaney to universalise the dilemma of artistic freedom by debating it outside an Irish context. Heaney's interest in Eastern European writers is not an abandonment of interest in those issues as a question for Irish writers, as he makes clear in the introductory essay to *The Government of the Tongue*: 'the relative absence of Irish subjects from this selection does not therefore mean lack of interest in what is happening in poetry on the home front or what is being made of it' (*GT* xx). The Eastern poets are, in Corcoran's terms, an 'exemplary' case, with application in Ireland as everywhere else.[5]

Mandelstam has been prominent in Heaney's poetry, both explicitly and implicitly, since 'Exposure' at the end of *North*. It is equally important, as I shall show, that he has a view of composition which is clearly akin to Heaney's concerns with 'phonetics and feeling' and the essential requirement of the local in the language of poetry. No poet could be more appropriate as a link between the book's two sections, forming the medial bridge between the miscellaneous essays on lyric poets, Western and Eastern, of Part I, and Part II's more sustained consideration of 'government' by and of poetry. In summarising the book's concerns at the end, Heaney recalls Mandelstam as a kind of *primus inter pares* of the book's poets, 'commending [him] for finding in Dante an example of unconstrained liberation' (*GT* 166). But to see him as no more than 'a first among equals' perhaps understates the centrality of this hybrid figure, Mandelstam's Dante, in the aesthetic of *The Government of the Tongue*, as well as Mandelstam's exemplary nature in Heaney's poetic generally.

Heaney goes on from the passage concerning the jurisdiction of the poet I quoted from the title-essay, to draw on his crucial discussion of Dante, 'Envies and Identifications: Dante and the Modern Poet'.[6] In this essay he argues that Dante has been 'all things to all poets', describing Yeats's post-Boccaccio lecherous Dante ('Ego Dominus Tuus'),[7] and Eliot's two Dantesque languages: the local, intimate forms of *The Waste Land* and the Latinate, imperial classicism of the *Four Quartets*.[8] It might seem surprising that this essay, which is one of Heaney's finest pieces of criticism, is not included whole in *The Government of the Tongue*. However, it is drawn on extensively at the start of the title-essay in developing Mandelstam's version of Dante, the figure of the imagining poet which is closest both to Heaney's heart and to his conception of the lyric poet. (Heaney's version of 'Dante the *lyric* poet', to which I return at the end, is summarised with impressive succinctness in Michael Parker's footnote 127, p. 267.)

There are two aspects of Mandelstam's Dante which appeal to

Heaney, and which he takes over. Indeed, Heaney's representation of Dante from Mandelstam's 'Conversation about Dante' is so selective that it might be more accurate to call it 'Heaney's Dante', particularly because it corresponds so well to his representations of other lyric poets (Kavanagh, for example). His characterisation of the 'Conversation' as 'a tumultuous affair' justifies this selectivity; Mandelstam's free association reads rather like a stream of Blakean aphorisms about literary creation.

To emphasise the appropriateness of Mandelstam's view of poetry to Heaney's requirements and temperament, we might note that Mandelstam's editors describe 'Conversation about Dante' as 'another attempt [by Mandelstam] to rephrase his views on the relationship of poetic craft, philology ... and ... poetry as an autonomous force in the universe'.[9] This could be taken over whole to characterise Heaney's poetics. Out of this extremely apposite welter Heaney selects four extracts to point up two ideas about the language of poetry. I will return to the relevance to Heaney of 'poetry as an autonomous force' towards the end of this chapter.

The first of the two formal, linguistic ideas highlighted by Heaney is Mandelstam's metaphorical characterisation of the *Commedia* as composed by the 'stereometric instinct' by which bees collaborate to build the solid geometry of the honeycomb. Dante's huge overall grasp of his conception is, according to the metaphor, less a product of rhetorical invention and disposition than an instinct like that by which bees co-operate to form combs, detail by detail, so that the honeycomb (the figure for the poem) seems to be built according to some internal dynamic without controlling exterior agency. Analogous ideas have been encountered repeatedly in Heaney's poetry in the foregoing pages here, from the inactive verbs and middle voice of *Station Island* onwards. Heaney includes Mandelstam's 'stereometric' idea as support for a general view of poetic inspiration, recognising 'instinct as its guiding principle' ('Envies and Identifications': 15): the vatic, divining notions of the poet which he has been keen to develop throughout his career, ever since 'Personal Helicon'.

But the second borrowed idea is even more important to Heaney (as it is to Mandelstam): the anti-Parnassian concentration on rough sound-production which is the local element in Dante, the parochial again. Mandelstam writes of the 'auditory coloration' of *Inferno* XXXII,[10] its 'peculiar labial music: "abbo" – "gabbo" – "babbo" – "Tebe" – "plebe" – "zebe" – "converrebbe". It's as if a nurse had participated in the creation of phonetics. Now the lips protrude in a childish manner, now they extend into a proboscis.'[11] This is inescapably reminiscent of Heaney's material phonetics, as well as the learning of language as a nursing process, from 'Death of a Naturalist' to 'Alphabets'.

Beyond the point where Heaney ends his extract, the passage in Mandelstam extends the phonetic description:

> The labials form some kind of 'numbered bass' . . .They are joined by . . . dental 'zz' and 'dz' sounds. . .Suddenly, for no apparent reason, a Slavic duck begins quacking: *Osteric, Tambernic, cric* (the onomatopoeic word for crackling). /The ice explodes phonetically. . . . A new link is revealed here between food and speech. . . The articulation of food and speech almost coincide.[12]

And Mandelstam goes on to quote the most masticatory parts of the second Ugolino canto, *Inferno* XXXIII – which, of course, Heaney translated at the end of *Field Work*.

Before returning to outline in detail Heaney's *ars poetica* as it emerges from *The Government of the Tongue* itself, two further Mandelstam parallels which bear on his aesthetic might be noted. In his 1922 essay, translated in Brown as 'On the Nature of the Word', Mandelstam stresses the centrality of 'philology' in literature: 'Philology is the family because every family clings to its own intonations, its personal references, and to its own special meanings of words defined in parentheses.'[13] After texts such as Paul de Man's 'Return to Philology'[14] we have slowly become accustomed in English to the European tradition of philological analysis (as distinct from its looser relation, New Critical 'practical criticism') as an indispensable tool in literary criticism. Heaney's criticism, in the tradition from Mandelstam, could be placed in the forefront of this process.

Secondly, we might note in passing the translator's use of the word 'decency' to represent what Mandelstam saw as a bourgeois fastidiousness which is inimical to the natural production of autonomous poetry.[15] The Joyce of 'Station Island', who advocates artistic freedom rather than 'doing the decent thing', has been said to be unJoycean; but he does have the excitable opinionatedness that characterises Mandelstam's critical flights.

The parallel is worth raising because Heaney's practice has never seemed to share, except as a wistful ideal, Stephen Dedalus's freedom-seeking indifference to 'decency' and responsibility. To redefine the Joycean ideal in relation to the case for naturalness rather than decency in Mandelstam's terms seems apt.

It is evident that what Heaney is assembling from several sources is the sense of poetry as physiologically determined, and therefore natural: an idea which is particularly prominent throughout Mandelstam's prose writings. What Mandelstam does with Dante, according to Heaney, 'is to bring him from the pantheon back to the palate' ('Envies and Identifications': 16). Heaney goes on to bring the two chosen elements of Mandelstam's Dante together: 'he possesses the poem as a musician possesses the score, both as a whole structure and as a sequence of delicious sounds' (*ibid*): that is, both the self-generating, 'stereometric' structure of the comb and the gustatory sweetness of the honey. And this third section of the Heaney essay ends by co-opting a constellation of the great poets as Heaney's Dante: '[Mandelstam's] Dante is a voluble Shakespearean figure, a woodcutter singing at his work in the dark wood of the larynx' ('Envies and Identifications': 18). (It is striking that, in reproducing this passage in *The Government of the Tongue*, Heaney expunges Shakespeare. This is not because he does not greatly revere him, but because Shakespeare would introduce a different consideration from the lyric poets. In the original essay the mention of Shakespeare arose as Eliot's contrast to the classical Dante, but now Heaney, following Mandelstam, has Dante performing this 'Shakespearean', non-classical function himself.)

The 'larynx' in this passage, surpassing in physical explicitness Mandelstam's metaphors, clearly belongs with the poetic metalanguage that Heaney himself has been developing since *Death of a Naturalist*. Obviously there are ways, too, in which Heaney is a very different kind of poet to Mandelstam, particularly in this matter of the materiality of his medium. I will return to this at the end of Section 3 below.

2. Government of and by the Tongue

Of all twentieth-century poets, Mandelstam can least be read without reference to the circumstances of the time in which he wrote. So in invoking his aesthetic, Heaney is also raising the association of the writer who was forced, finally, in his poetry to oppose the political realities around him. When we turn to *The Government of the Tongue* itself, and its concerns – accepting that Edward Mendelson, in his *Times Literary Supplement* review, was right in seeing them as more integrated than Heaney claims – the question we are forced to ask is: what is it about poetry that gives it this Shelleyan right to govern? Heaney has always by nature been tempted to pass up this right, for a quiet life: to 'let it go', as he said in 'An Open Letter', or to withdraw conveniently into the male reticence of his Ulster background. 'My temper is not Brechtian', he said to Melvyn Bragg in the 'South Bank Show' interview. In this way, 'the government of the tongue', as Heaney says, is an apt title because it can mean either government *by* the tongue or the governing *of* the tongue, in the sense of holding it in check.

This question is raised in Heaney's strange moral reminiscence which comes at the beginning of *The Government of the Tongue*, at the start of an essay which stands in a kind of privileging Limbo outside the book's two Parts (like the translations of Virgil and Dante in *Seeing Things*). It is the story of the cancellation of a recording session by Heaney and his friend David Hammond out of deference to the seriousness of a bombing in Belfast. Ought Heaney and Hammond to have gone on with the motley, their poems and songs, within earshot of the sirens of the ambulances and fire engines? In the event they adopted the humane course, did what Heaney calls in the Joyce poem of 'Station Island' 'the decent thing', and went home. But the story prepares the way for a consideration of the circumstances where the tongue *could* – or even should – sing out, regardless of consequence or constraint. What determines whether the tongue is to govern or be governed?

The implicit concern with the relative weight to be given to artistic and political imperatives is made explicit in the title-lecture in Part II, so the central issue is raised in the introductory section to each Part. The title-lecture goes on to develop the more immediate sense of the title (as in the colloquial 'hold your tongue!'), principally by reference to the Polish poet Zbigniew Herbert, whose poem 'A Knocker' – on the surface, at least – is sceptical about poetry's right to any special status (*GT* 99–100). As so often in all his writing, both in poetry and prose, Heaney is exploiting the ambiguity of his title, its 'doubleness': the doubt which, in his review of *The Government of the Tongue*, John Carey sees as inescapable in Heaney.[16]

There is a temporary resolution of doubt when Heaney comes down decisively on the side of poetic autonomy here, notably in this sentence, which recalls Mandelstam's 'poetry as an auton-omous force in the universe':

> The fact is that poetry is its own reality and no matter how much a poet may concede to the corrective pressures of social, moral, political and historical reality, the ultimate fidelity must be to the demands and promise of the artistic event. (*GT* 101)

He restates this judgement at the very end of the last lecture on Sylvia Plath, when he returns to 'the general theme of these lectures, submerged as the theme may have been for much of the time' (*GT* 166), to conclude:

> I do not in fact see how poetry can survive as a category of human consciousness if it does not put poetic considerations first – expressive considerations, that is, based upon its own genetic laws which spring into operation at the moment of lyric conception. (*GT* 166)

The last phrase is Heaney's most precise formulation of the notion of poetic composition that has been developing throughout his career. The confidence of its expression here parallels another Mandelstam metaphor for Dante's *Commedia*, taken from crystal-lography. The genetic laws '*spring*', unwilled, into operation 'at the moment of lyric *conception*' (emphases added): they are completely operative at that moment, like crystals which form spontaneously in a solution. This metaphor from nature reinforces an observation about Shakespeare made by Heaney in 'Envies and Identifications', following on from Eliot's contrast of the 'univer-sal language' of Dante with Shakespeare's 'intelligibility and remoteness', which are untranslatable because they are local rather than universal. Heaney changes Eliot's characterisation of Shakespeare, while claiming to rephrase it: 'The poetry, in other words, is to a large extent in the phonetics, in the genetic energies of English words' ('Envies and Identifications': 11). This summary is not, in fact, what Eliot said; but then Heaney often agrees less with Eliot than his sense of Eliot's status as modern master allows him to admit.[17]

While *The Government of the Tongue*, then, follows *Preoccupations* in claiming for poetry the right to artistic freedom, the rationale for it, which was inchoate in the earlier book, is now founded on a more secure theoretical basis. Mandelstam, particularly in his 'Conversation about Dante', has offered a view of poetry in which the formal, the local and the politically urgent are all catered for, while still claiming autonomy for poetry itself. This insistence on the autonomy of poetry has to be seen in the context of something I noted at the start, which is even more fundamental to Heaney's criticism but too obvious to have been given much attention: the sustained centrality of lyric poetry as his topic. Perhaps no critic since Dante in the *Convivio* and the *Vita Nuova* has made lyric poetry so solely his concern (Heaney's *Monarchia*, his definition of what the well-ordered political state would be, is still to come, perhaps). Like Dante, Heaney is not devoted to criticism for its own sake; he is a glossator or commentator (Dante's *chiosatore*) on the writing of lyric. In 'Envies and Identifications' he remarks that the 'essentially lyric' Dante he is developing with Mandelstam 'is stripped of the robes of commentary in which he began to vest himself with his epistle to Can Grande' (16). In other contexts, too, Heaney is by no means indifferent to the power and importance of Dante as commentator. His public lectures on poetry show him to be an exceptionally attentive and subtle close reader of poets of all periods: Clare, Herbert, Hopkins, Bishop.

This absolute concentration on lyric poetry in his criticism (there is no Shakespeare, for example) is crucial, because it explains why Heaney comes down in this context so firmly on the side of poetic autonomy against political art. What he is attempting to do is to define lyric poetry itself, to say what kind of *thing* it is. This is essential, because high claims are being made for it. What is this force which is claiming the 'right to govern' and legislate for readers? Only when we know that can we go on to debate its function and areas of application. Hence the odd, apparently grandiose phrase quoted above, 'a category of human consciousness' (*GT* 166), a phrase which takes us back again to the Aristotelian, categorical world of the *Vita Nuova*.

In fact Heaney is thinking of something quite specific in this phrase, something which is a perennial concern of his. In a very insightful short essay in the first half of this book, 'The Impact of Translation', he indicates what this 'category of human consciousness' is. He warns that the reader of a translation is experiencing something 'radically and logically different' from the reader of a poem in the original, because 'phonetics and feeling [are] so intimately related in the human make-up' (*GT* 39). This recalls the second sense of 'tongue' in the quotation about language's right to govern: 'the common resource of language itself'. Poetry is the direct, unwilled expression of the language itself, a 'category of consciousness' which is nearly unconscious. Its sound may be more revealing than its meaning, as a more direct, unmediated expression of the language which exists (according to a Saussurean paradox) as a structure independent of any one use of it.

Criticism of Heaney has taken note of this aural bias. Both Anthony Thwaite in his *Times Literary Supplement* review of *Preoccupations*[18] and Anne Stevenson in her discussion of it (Curtis 131–7) cite Eliot's 'auditory imagination' to describe this emphasis in Heaney, and it is a central element in Elmer Andrews's *The Poetry of Seamus Heaney*, as its subtitle, 'All the Realms of Whisper', suggests.[19] But to take seriously Eliot's theory of the auditory imagination (*P* 150), as a pre-expressive sense of form, is to raise very difficult critical questions. It requires some kind of formalist criticism, something to which the English tradition has been very resistant. The only critic who has read Heaney much in this way is the French formalist scholar Adolphe Haberer, whose reading of 'Gifts of Rain'[20] employs a formalist phonetic method overingeniously, but has the distinct merit of taking the 'auditory imagination' seriously. Everyone admires Heaney's theory of the originary ooze in the Hopkins essay, but Haberer seems to be the only critic who extends the idea into his own practice.

Eliot's theory of the auditory imagination has much in common with Mandelstam's poetic based on 'philology', with the radical difference that Eliot, in his 'Milton I' essay,[21] worries about the adverse effects of its 'hypertrophy', while Mandelstam sees it as the essence of the poetic enterprise. Heaney employs Eliot's term, but in a sense closer to Mandelstam's, seeing poetry as utterance by 'the language itself', using the poet as medium. It is a development of the notion which Heaney, in a striking piece of defamiliarising, had called 'technique' rather than 'craft' in his famous distinction in the essay 'Feeling into Words' in *Preoccupations* (47 ff.). It had been put quite expressly at the start of the following essay in *Preoccupations*, 'The Makings of a Music':

> What interests me is the relationship between the almost physiological operations of a poet composing and the music of the finished poem. (*P* 61)

'Physiological' is putting it very strongly, laying great weight on the chemistry of the poem's production. This, too, bears an interesting relationship to the process of poetry production outlined by Dante and his school, the *stilnovisti* of thirteenth-century Tuscany. They similarly believed that the poem's cause was a physiological, materialist process. Cavalcante's 'Donna mi prega' is the fullest exposition of how the sight of the beloved sets up in the mind of the observer a condition that naturally issues as poetry.[22]

Heaney's theory is impressively realised in critical practice in *The Government of the Tongue*, in two essays on writers who do not seem to concern themselves directly with the poet's obligations at all: Elizabeth Bishop, in Heaney's brilliant practical-critical reading of 'At the Fishhouses' in the book's title-lecture, and Sylvia Plath. It is immediately evident from the Plath poem to which Heaney gives most prominence (it provides the title for his last lecture) that she is being seen as exemplary of Heaney's materialist definition of lyric as physio-/phonologically induced. That poem, 'Words', encapsulates to a remarkable degree the elements of Heaney's *ars poetica*: language is imaged chemically as the sap (the Shakespearian 'ooze' of the Hopkins essay) rising through the wood which 'rings' at the axe-stroke to produce 'echoes' that travel out from the centre, like the publication of the finished poem.

Plath's poem is more obscure than I am suggesting, especially in its ending, where the fixed stars at the bottom of the pool 'govern a life'. But even this fits Heaney's poetic. The word 'govern' finds its place as the conclusion of Heaney's 'Government' of the tongue, and implicitly reinforces his view: the finished poem may indeed 'govern a life'; it may have a public impact. But that stage is separate from its origins. The poem's aptness for Heaney's view of the origin of lyric makes it unsurprising that Andrew Motion calls this lecture by Heaney 'one of the masterpieces of modern criticism'.[23] Hence the two main elements in Heaney's *ars poetica* come together. It is precisely because the poem is produced by a formal phonological process that it has to be seen as, in essence, independent of exterior circumstance.

Two other poetic manifestos to which Heaney feels sympathetic are quoted in the course of *The Government of the Tongue*; both bear on the question of poetic autonomy. The most famous is one which Heaney has cited before: Archibald MacLeish's 'A poem should not mean/ But be'. This is the most celebrated statement in English of poetry's claim to autonomy, and to natural utterance. It is close to Lowell's, which Heaney both quotes and echoes: 'A poem is an event, not the record of an event' (or, indeed, Beckett's saying of *Finnegans Wake* that it is 'not about something: it is that thing itself').

But the most significant manifesto for Heaney is Milosz's poem 'Ars Poetica'. Though it shares a name with MacLeish's, it is opposed to his view of poetry in every other way:

> In the very essence of poetry there is something indecent:
> a thing is brought forth which we didn't know we had in us.
>
> (*GT* 166)

However, while this attitude is troubled by poetry's moral irresponsibility (which is 'indecent': we recall again Mandelstam, as well as Heaney's Joyce and the escape from 'doing the decent thing'), it suggests a similar chemical origin. These are views of the poetic imagination with which Heaney agrees, held in balance though they are by his characterisation of Herbert's poetic: 'Enjoy poetry as long as you don't use it to escape reality' (*GT* xix). If Heaney has seemed, on balance, to come down on the side of poetic freedom in this book, we should remember that his first Oxford lecture on poetry two years later would be entitled 'The Redress of Poetry', arguing that the private and public imperatives must be kept in balance.[24]

Heaney's own poetic is a variation on these themes. While I

have claimed that his familiarity with Mandelstam associates him with a world outside the norms of English criticism, there is a homelier comparison that might be made: with Housman's linking of the production of poetry to the digestive system. Milosz's poem concludes with the hope that 'good spirits will choose us for their instrument'. Heaney wants good language to choose the poet for its instrument.

The first reactions to *The Government of the Tongue* mostly admired its commitment to the importance of art. Any reservations that were expressed had to do with the language of Heaney's criticism. For example, Derick Thomson says that in the essay on Auden, Heaney 'launches into a torrent of phonological, grammatical and psychological interpretation';[25] Stephen Logan, in a hard-hitting but amusing review in the *Spectator*, found disturbing 'a tendency towards grandiloquence'.[26] It is clear that both of these charges can be answered by reference to Mandelstam's type of criticism and the return to philology. (That is not to say, of course, that one may not still dislike that kind of criticism; but it suggests a parallel which shows that it is not an unconsidered tic which Heaney indulges unconsciously.) As Colm Tóibin said: 'It is as though he needs to insist that he is not a critic, or a prose-writer, but a poet trying to clear space for himself ... willing to take the risk.'[27] Heaney likes 'chancy' critics as well as chancy poets.

The riskiness of this kind of criticism is clearly characteristic of the poet-critic rather than the work of the critical academy, and Heaney is recognised as the leading representative of this kind of criticism in contemporary English poetry. This connects him not only with Mandelstam but also with the mainstream English critical-theoretical tradition since Coleridge's theory of the imagination, seeing lyric poets as conditioned by a set of linguistic and material circumstances that are instinctive and above rational control. His practice of letting the language lead etymologically where it wants, in a manner curiously akin to deconstructive criticism (poetic line and military line, home/Homer, and so on (*GT* xv and 6)') can be seen in this tradition too. Likewise, his sense that 'phonetics and feelings [are] so intimately related in the human make-up' (*GT* 39) – that the fact will emerge at whatever point poetic expression is tested – might be seen in relation to Romantic theories of organicism. The reason for Heaney's preferred concentration on Dante and the East European poets as poet-critic predecessors is the more explicit sense of public reality that is incorporated in their poetics.

3. Dante and Natural Language

Heaney, as he claims all Dante-influenced poets do, seizes enthusiastically on the features of Mandelstam's Dante which he finds congenial. Dante is the great 'inner émigré', the poet of the Ovidian *tristia* of the exile, famously lamenting how salt-bitter is the taste of foreign food, and how weary the ascent of foreign stairs. Heaney associates his retreat to Wicklow with Mandelstam's banishment to Voronezh and Dante's to Ravenna. Mandelstam's Gothic Dante – the rough-hewn poet of parochial dialect[28] – and his view of Dante's great poetic structure as something which forms by its own internal logic are both very much to Heaney's purpose.

I have stressed throughout this book the ways in which Heaney's approach is calculated, comparing this to Yeats's 'cunning' in finding and using materials which are to his purpose: 'something here for me', as Heaney says in the O'Driscoll interview on *Sweeney Astray*.[29] He builds on his affinity with Mandelstam. But if Heaney and Mandelstam share a notion of the source of poetry, physiologically and structurally, they are very different poets too, with very different temperaments.

There are features of Dante which come straight to Heaney, without Mandelstam's intermediacy. The most obvious example is the moral cosmology of Dante's afterlife which Heaney adopts in *Station Island*, without a parallel in Mandelstam. Second – and more important for a consideration of language – is the principle of local language from *De Vulgari Eloquentia*, discussed above. Dante's is the most memorable claim for naturalness in poetic utterance, a claim that lies behind such aspirations as Wordsworth's towards the language of 'a man speaking to men' in the Preface to *The Lyrical Ballads*, or Yeats's to express his passions, or Lowell's to 'say what happened'. In Canto XXIV of *Purgatorio*, Bonagiunta da Lucca, an Italian poet of the generation immediately before Dante, pays him the greatest compliment he receives in his afterworld journey, asking to be told 'if I see here the one who

composed those new rhymes which begin *"Donne ch'avete
intelletto d'amore"'* (XXIV, 49–51). Dante replies with one of the
greatest poetic statements:

> I' mi son un che, quando
> Amor mi spira, noto, e a quel modo
> ch'e' ditta dentro vo significando.
> (52–4)[30]

('I am one who, when passion inspires me, take note of it and
proceed to express it exactly in the way it said.') My translation
fails to bring out the 'phonetics as feeling' idea in the Dante: the
poet sets about 'signifying' directly what passion 'said', in the
same 'mode'.

Many of Heaney's most urgent poetic statements are encapsu-
lated here: 'description is revelation'; to dig the truth with the pen
or to plumb its wells; above all to achieve in writing the clarity of
the 'bleb of the icicle'. Dante is claiming clarity of language, in
transcribing the dictates of passion without the intermediacy of
calculating form. It has to be repeated, of course, that there is no
such language. The aspiration is towards a representational
poetic: a metaphor for translating event into word. This ideal
could be seen as the attempt to capture in writing the apparently
immediate representationalism of spoken language, especially
local dialect.

Heaney's addition to the long tradition of this metaphor is
almost to despair of poetry's capacity to devise a rhetoric which
can represent passion directly by a 'natural' process. Hence his
roughness of diction (something of which Dante stood accused for
centuries) as a calculated slight to the claims of more decorous
language ('and so on'); his tropes of inexpressibility ('that last /gh
the strangers found/ difficult to manage'); the reluctant embracing
of transparent metrical forms and avoidance of more expressive
but arcane ones; the grammatical forms that imply non-agency in
the production of writing (the intransitives, passives and partici-
ples); his retreat into what Hart calls deconstruction: the global
'O' at the end of *The Haw Lantern*'s 'Alphabets' in place of more
'meaningful' language.

The paradox is that it is precisely this recognition of the
impossibility of unmediated language that gives Heaney's poetry

its characteristic force and precision. Moreover, it carries the implication that his subject – 'doing the decent thing' – has prior importance as what needed to be expressed. This theme of difficulty is the reason why the dismantling of his language is the most essential prerequisite to an understanding of his significance as a poet, as Dante was, of the contemporary political condition.

But – to return finally to language again – the greatest appeal for Heaney in Dante is his most extraordinary quality as a poet: the way he is epic and lyric poet at once. For Heaney, Dante is the epic of the parish, as Homer was for Yeats. In his consideration of the aesthetics of the lyric, Heaney is unable to consider Shakespeare and Joyce. Apart from the large-scale use of Dante as a structural parallel in *Station Island* and in translations which resonate with contemporary concerns (as Ugolino parallels the IRA hunger-strikers, or Charon figures the various *rites de passage* with which *Seeing Things* is absorbed), Dante is used increasingly as the great lyric exemplar. The compelling aspect of Dante for Heaney is the way the local precision and evocativeness of an imagist poet are used within an overall imaginative scheme of which the particular images are expressions. F.R. Leavis felicitously called Milton's similes in *Paradise Lost* 'smuggled-in pieces of imaginative indulgence'. Dante's images are more integrated than this, but it does suggest how the detail enhances the larger structure. Of all poets, he is the greatest exponent of the perfect detailed image with 'axiomatic rightness' (to use again Foster's formula for Heaney).

The detailed references in Heaney move in the opposite direction: for example, in 'Sandstone Keepsake' the seashore stone is compared to the hotbed of Phlegethon of *Inferno* XII (*SI* 20). The association works outwards to consider his 'free state of image and illusion'. Similarly, the sound of a twig snapping in 'The Loaning' is moved towards universality by the association with Piero delle Vigne in *Inferno* XIII[31] (*SI* 52). A larger-scale authority is claimed by the association, just as the collections of shorter lyrics in *Field Work*, *Station Island* and *Seeing Things* aspire towards something like an epic scale of overall coherence by association with Dante in the translations they include. In the same way, a large political perspective is gained by Dantesque associations in 'Crossings' xxxvi (*ST* 94) and the *terza rima* of 'From the Frontier of Writing' in *The Haw Lantern* (6). It is Dante above all who provides the larger scope, in language, politics and ethics, that warrants Heaney's making such great claims for the jurisdiction of poetry.

Conclusion

Where do we place Heaney on the basis of this linguistic analysis? Throughout his career several general identifications have been made. *Death of a Naturalist* was co-opted into the anti-Movement school of Hughes, with its deliberately roughened textures as recommended by Hobsbaum. There is no doubt, I think, that, well as that book was received, the roughening went against the natural grain in Heaney. When he moved towards smoother forms in *Field Work*, Alvarez accused him of selling out on the new practices and recidivising into the 'gentility principle' that Alvarez himself, in the campaigning Preface to his *New Poetry* in 1962, had seen as a deplorable feature of the Movement poets. This charge, though we see its formal meaning, now looks particularly absurd when we consider the great sombre elegies in *Field Work*: 'Casualty', 'After a Killing' and 'The Strand at Lough Beg'. Nobody would now see any of the poems in *Death of a Naturalist* as comparable in seriousness with them, however formally regular their expression.

There is less difficulty, I think, in saying what Heaney is not. Like both the Movement poets and the Hughes generation, he is not a modernist. His temper is constructive, not iconoclastic. Even the Poundean urge to go against 'the tyranny of the iamb' was not natural to him, and was not sustained. Besides, the less campaigning modernism of Eliot is not to his taste either, although Eliot's classicism, with its strong sense of tradition, is; Eliot's 'Tradition and the Individual Talent' has probably had more impact on his critical model than any other predecessor. In many ways I think Heaney's passing discussion of Eliot's Dante in 'Envies and Identifications' (discussed in Chapter 5) gives as much clue to the essence of his own aesthetic philosophy as anything he writes. For example, his puzzlement that Eliot did not make more of the Guelf/Ghibelline side of Dante – his reconciliation of Church and State – is itself puzzling: Eliot's political-cultural pronouncements were never very revealing. But the point is, Heaney's *are* revealing. The frequent references to Eliot in *The Government of the Tongue* are not only a courtesy because he is giving the Eliot Lectures; Heaney sees Eliot, both as modernist and as arch-conservative, as still the most formidable and distinguished literary-political antagonist of the era.

But no one has thought of Heaney as a modernist. He has been called, with increasing frequency, a postmodernist. Again, there is some formal support for this. Henry Hart sees *The Haw Lantern* as a deconstructive book (for brevity here I am taking the two categories together: I am aware that they are distinct), beginning with the analysis of 'Alphabets' as scriptist: that is, on the side of the Derridean case for writing against logocentrism. But this is to generalise too much; throughout his career Heaney's language has been strongly informed by spoken forms. Even if that were more true of *Death of a Naturalist* than of *Seeing Things*, it would be perverse to characterise as hostile to spoken usage a poet as locally rooted in his language as Heaney. Hart points out, rightly, that Heaney is familiar with the terms of deconstruction (difference, and so on) and makes play with them. Similarly, Stan Smith, at the beginning of his essay in *The Chosen Ground*, notes (not entirely with approval: he calls it 'a tic of rhetorical routine') Heaney's tendency in his criticism, from an early stage in his career, to play with deconstructive etymological puns: for example, 'feeling into words', or 'sense of place'. There are many examples in *The Government of the Tongue*: Owen 'earned the right to his lines by going up the line' (xv); 'Homer . . . home' (6); *persona* derived from *personare*, 'to sound out through' (149). And there is the occasional recognisably postmodernist poem, such as 'Serenades' (*WO*), 'Somnambulist' (*WO*), and the much-anthologised, Muldonian (and dedicated to Muldoon) 'Widgeon' (*SI*).

But that is not Heaney's characteristic poetic world either. Indeed, I think Smith's reservation is partly based on a sense, which I share, that it does not really suit Heaney. The fact is that, uniconoclastic and classically inclined though he is, his poetry breaks new ground in English. The nearest thing to a predecessor, perhaps, is Auden; but Heaney is obviously unlike Auden in important ways. His novelty is partly attributable to the incorporation of Irish subjects and – to a lesser extent – forms into his usage. But Fennell is right, as far as that goes, to say that Heaney does not always write as an Irish poet, which would surely be a disabling constraint. His novelty lies more in his borrowing from Eastern European poets, especially Mandelstam, a language and forms to address public issues.

To quote again one of Heaney's most important aphorisms: 'a formal choice is never simply formal'. The leaning towards clarity in style, to aspire to a transparency which will be of public utility (his 'present use'), sometimes faces up to the need for a colloquialism in usage which traditionally has been acceptable only in translation ('illumination, and so on'). It is significant that there is not yet a 'school of Heaney'; we do not yet see his achievement as a whole. And no doubt it will be some time before we do. The capacity in him to change, noted by Deane, Vendler and others, entitles him to our trust. Like the friends appealed to by Yeats in a quatrain quoted above, we must not mistake the issue at stake in the formal choices he is constantly reviewing: 'It is myself that I remake.' And the self that he remakes is, above all, the exemplary poet who has, in Leavis's formula, given evidence 'that he has been fully alive in our time'.

Notes

Introduction: 'An art that knows its mind'

1. *The Redress of Poetry. An Inaugural Lecture delivered before the University of Oxford on 24 October 1989* (Oxford: Clarendon Press, 1989), 1.
2. Michael Parker, *Seamus Heaney: The Making of the Poet* (Dublin: Gill & Macmillan, 1993). Hereafter referenced in the text as 'Parker'.
3. John Carey, 'Poetry for the World We Live in' (*The Sunday Times*, 18 November 1979), 40.
4. Desmond Fennell, *Whatever You Say, Say Nothing: Why Seamus Heaney is No. 1* (Dublin: ELO Publications, 1991).
5. David Lloyd, '"Pap for the Dispossessed": Seamus Heaney and the Poetics of Identity' (*Boundary*, 2 [Winter 1985], 319–42). Reprinted in Elmer Andrews (ed.), *Seamus Heaney: A Collection of Critical Essays* (London: Macmillan, 1992), 87–116.
6. 'To be able to use the first person singular to mean *me*', from a letter to Brian Friel, quoted in many places including an interview with James Randall in *Ploughshares*, 5, 3 (1979), 7–22.
7. Henry Hart, *Seamus Heaney: Poet of Contrary Progressions* (New York: Syracuse University Press, 1992). Hereafter referenced in the text as 'Hart'.
8. For example, R. Jakobson, *Language in Literature*, eds K. Pomorska and S. Rudy (Cambridge, MA and London: Harvard University Press, 1987); Antony Easthope, *Poetry as Discourse* (London and New York: Methuen, 1983).

9. Stan Smith's confident and enlightening account of Yeats's syntax is an impressive recent exception, in *W.B. Yeats: A Critical Introduction* (Savage, MD: Barnes & Noble, 1990), 122–52.

10. '"The Fire i' the Flint". Reflections on the Poetry of Gerard Manley Hopkins' (British Academy Chatterton Lecture, 1974). Reprinted in *Preoccupations: Selected Prose 1968–78* (London: Faber & Faber, 1980), 81.

11. Neil Corcoran, *English Poetry since 1940* (London and New York: Longman, 1993), 183.

12. Edna Longley, '"Inner Emigré" or "Artful Voyeur"?', in Tony Curtis (ed.), *The Art of Seamus Heaney* (Bridgend Poetry Wales Press, 2nd edn, 1985), 87. I have drawn on Curtis a good deal, especially for this important essay, so it is referenced hereafter as 'Curtis' in the text.

13. Blake Morrison, *Seamus Heaney* (London: Methuen, 1982), 19. This study made an admirable start to extended consideration of Heaney from which criticism of him has never looked back. Referenced hereafter as 'Morrison' in the text.

14. *The New Poetry*, selected and introduced by A. Alvarez (Harmondsworth: Penguin, 1962), 17 ff.

15. Seamus Deane, *A Short History of Irish Literature* (London: Hutchinson, 1986), 241.

16. Haffenden, 64.

17. Randall interview; see note 6 above, 21.

18. *The Variorum Edition of the Poems of W.B. Yeates.* eds Peter Allt and Russell K. Alspach (New York: Macmillan, 1956), 778.

19. Antony Easthope, 'Transparency as Explicit Ideal', in *Poetry as Discourse* (London and New York: Methuen, 1983), 110.

20. *Cencrastus* (Autumn 1988), 51.

21. For example, Jakobson, *Language in Literature*; see note 8 above, 198–249.

22. Thomas C. Foster, *Seamus Heaney* (Dublin: The O'Brien Press, 1989), 140.

23. Elmer Andrews, *The Poetry of Seamus Heaney: All the Realms of Whisper* (London: Macmillan, 1988), 203.

24. J.W. Foster, 'The Poetry of Seamus Heaney' (*Critical Quarterly*, 16, 1 [Spring 1974]), 48.

25. Alan Robinson, *Instabilities in Contemporary British Poetry* (London: Macmillan, 1988), 125: 'There is something insidious about the way in which the iambic base rhythm effortlessly accommodates atrocities.'

26. *'Among Schoolchildren': A John Malone Memorial Lecture.* Thursday 9 June 1983, Queen's University Belfast (Belfast: The John Malone Memorial Committee, 1983).

27. J.R. Lawlor (ed.), *Paul Valéry: An Anthology* (London: Routledge & Kegan Paul, 1977): 'Poetry as Abstract Thought', 155.
28. Seamus Deane, 'Interview with Seamus Heaney', *The Crane Bag*, 1, 1 (1977); reprinted in M. P. Hederman and R. Kearney (eds) *The Crane Bag Book of Irish Studies (1977–1981)* (Dublin: Blackwater Press, 1982), 70.
29. *YP* 79.
30. John Montague, *The Rough Field* (Dublin: Dolmen, 1972; reprinted Newcastle upon Tyne: Bloodaxe, 1990).
31. Robert Welch, *Changing States: Transformations in Modern Irish Writing* (London: Routledge, 1993), 253.
32. F.R. Leavis, *New Bearings in English Poetry: A Study of the Contemporary Situation* (London: Chatto & Windus, 1932; 2nd edn 1950), 24.
33. Edward Broadbridge, *Seamus Heaney* (Copenhagen: Danmarksradio, Skolaradioen, 1977), n.p.
34. Interview with Melvyn Bragg after the publication of *Seeing Things*, 'South Bank Show', Sunday 27 October 1991.
35. Robert Lowell, 'Epilogue', in *Day by Day* (London: Faber & Faber, 1978), 127.
36. C.C. O'Brien, 'A Slow North-East Wind' (*The Listener*, 25 September 1975), 404–5.
37. Neil Corcoran, 'Quickened into Verb' (*PN Review* 31, 1983, 9, 5), 69.
38. Robert Farren, *The Course of Irish Verse* (London: Sheed & Ward, 1948), 57–61.
39. T.S. Eliot, 'Milton I', in *On Poetry and Poets* (London: Faber & Faber, 1957), 143. Originally published 1936.

Chapter I   English or Irish Lyric? (1960s Heaney)

1. For Morrison, Corcoran, Andrews and Tamplin, see Bibliography.
2. *The Penguin Book of Contemporary British Poetry*, eds Blake Morrison and Andrew Motion (Harmondsworth: Penguin, 1982), 17.
3. Desmond Fennell, see note 4 in Introduction above.
4. T.S. Eliot, 'Tradition and the Individual Talent', in *Selected Essays* (3rd edn, London: Faber & Faber, 1951), 13–22. Originally published 1919.
5. Neil Corcoran, 'Seamus Heaney and the Art of the Exemplary' (*Yearbook of English Studies*, 17 [1987]), 120.

6. Seamus Heaney, *An Open Letter* (A Field Day Pamphlet, Number 2, Derry, 1983), stanza 33.

7. Morrison and Motion (eds) *The Penguin Book of Contemporary British Poetry*, 13.

8. W.H. Auden, *Collected Longer Poems* (London: Faber & Faber, 1968), 35–76; John Fuller, *Epistles to Several Persons* (London: Secker & Warburg, 1973).

9. Seamus Deane (ed.), *The Field Day Anthology of Irish Writing* (Derry: Field Day, 1992), III, 1314–15.

10. Broadbridge, see note 33 to Introduction here.

11. W.B. Yeats, *Essays and Introductions* (London: Macmillan, 1961), 520.

12. '*Among Schoolchildren*', see note 26 to Introduction above.

13. Farren, p. 57: see note 38 to Introduction above.

14. Austin Clarke, *Poetry in Modern Ireland* (Cork: Mercier Press, 2nd edn, n.d.), 43.

15. Robert Welch, *A History of Verse Translation from the Irish 1789–1897* (Gerrards Cross, Bucks.: Colin Smythe, 1988), 160.

16. W.B. Yeats, 'What is Popular Poetry?' (1901), in *Essays and Introductions*, 3.

17. *ibid.*, 5.

18. Thomas MacDonagh, *Literature in Ireland: Studies Irish and Anglo-Irish* (London: T. Fisher Unwin, 1916), 64–82.

19. W.B. Yeats, *The Collected Plays of W.B. Yeats* (London: Macmillan, 2nd edn, 1952), 177.

20. *YP* 350, (quoted Smith, 128: see note 9 to Introduction above.)

21. Austin Clarke, *Collected Poems* (Dublin: Dolmen Press, 1974), 162, as 'The Scholar'.

22. *ibid.*, 173.

23. Paul Muldoon, *Why Brownlee Left* (London: Faber & Faber, 1980), 22.

24. Loreto Todd, *The Language of Irish Literature* (London: Macmillan, 1989), 105.

25. *ibid.*, 115.

26. Colin Meir, *The Ballads and Songs of W.B. Yeats* (London: Macmillan, 1974), 78 ff.

27. W.B. Yeats, 'An Acre of Grass', *YP* 420.

28. T.R. Henn, *The Lonely Tower: Studies in the Poetry of W.B. Yeats* (London: Methuen, 2nd edn, 1965), 113.

29. *YP*, 380.

30. Paul Fussell in W.K. Wimsatt (ed.), *Versification: Major Language Types* (New York: New York University Press, 1972), 197.

31. Thomas Kinsella, *The New Oxford Book of Irish Verse* (Oxford: Oxford University Press, 1986), xxvii.

32. Seamus Deane, 'Interview with Seamus Heaney', in M.P. Hederman and R. Kearney (eds), *The Crane Bag Book of Irish Studies (1977–1981)*, (Dublin: Blackwater Press, 1982), 69.
33. *ibid.*, 66.
34. *Coriolanus*, V, vi, 113–15, in G.B. Evans (ed.), *The Riverside Shakespeare* (Boston, MA: Houghton Mifflin, 1974), 1436.
35. Lowell, see note 35 to Introduction here.
36. Daniel Corkery, *The Hidden Ireland* (Dublin: Gill & Macmillan, 2nd edn, 1925), 79.
37. Dante, *Purgatorio* XXIV, 52–4.
38. Helen Vendler, *The Music of What Happens: Poems, Poets, Critics* (Cambridge, MA and London: Harvard University Press, 1988).
39. Keith Walker (ed.), *John Dryden* (Oxford, 'Oxford Authors': Oxford University Press, 1987), 219–27.
40. Stan Smith, 'The Distance Between: Seamus Heaney', in Neil Corcoran (ed.), *The Chosen Ground: Essays on the Contemporary Poetry of Northern Ireland* (Bridgend: Seren Books, 1992), 51.
41. Ezra Pound, *The Cantos of Ezra Pound* (London: Faber & Faber, 1954), Canto 81, 553.
42. Patrick Kavanagh, *The Complete Poems*, collected, arranged and ed. Peter Kavanagh (Newbridge, Co. Kildare: The Goldsmith Press, 1984), 18.
43. *ibid.*, 13.
44. Smith, 'The Distance Between'; see note 40 above, 36 ff.
45. J.W. Foster, 'The Poetry of Seamus Heaney' (see note 24 to Introduction here). 41.
46. *Times Literary Supplement*, 4722 (1 October 1993), 5.
47. Reprinted as Terence Brown, 'A Northern Voice', in H. Bloom (ed.), *Seamus Heaney: Modern Critical Views* (New York: Chelsea House, 1986), 25 ff. Originally 'Four New Voices: Poetry of the Present', in *Northern Voices: Poets from Ulster* (Dublin: Gill & Macmillan, 1975).
48. T.S. Eliot, 'Little Gidding', in *The Complete Poems and Plays* (London: Faber & Faber, 1969), 194.
49. For a succinct account of Jakobson's constituent elements, see Linda R. Waugh, 'The Poetic Function and the Nature of Language', in R. Jakobson, *Verbal Art, Verbal Sign, Verbal Time*, eds K. Pomorska and S. Rudy (Oxford: Blackwell, 1977), 143–68.
50. Michael Allen's review of *The Haw Lantern* in *The Irish Review*, 3 (1988) 108–18; reprinted, with minor changes, as '"Holding Course": *The Haw Lantern* and its Place in Heaney's Development', in Elmer Andrews (ed.) *Seamus Heaney: A Collection of Critical Essays* (London: Macmillan, 1992), 195.

51. Seamus Deane, *A Short History of Irish Literature* (London: Hutchinson, 1986), 240.
52. *Preoccupations*, 37.
53. Neil Corcoran, *English Poetry since 1940* (London and New York: Longman, 1993), 182.
54. Randall interview, 18–19; see note 6 to Introduction.

Chapter 2 Phonetics and Feeling: *Wintering Out, North* and *Field Work* (1970s Heaney)

1. Neil Corcoran, *English Poetry since 1940* (see note 53 to Chapter 1), 182.
2. *ibid.*, 196.
3. Seamus Heaney, interview with Elgy Gillespie, *The Irish Times*, 19 May 1972, 'A Political Stance'.
4. Tom McArthur, *Oxford Companion to the English Language* (Oxford: Oxford University Press, 1992).
5. James Joyce, *A Portrait of the Artist as a Young Man* (Harmondsworth: Penguin, 1992), 205.
6. P.W. Joyce, *Irish Local Names Explained* (Dublin, 1923: reprinted London: Fitzhouse Books, 1990), 49.
7. Brian Friel, *Translations* (London: Faber & Faber, 1981).
8. *YP* 347.
9. Seamus Heaney interview with Seamus Deane, (see note 28 to Introduction here), 70.
10. D.F. McCarthy, Introduction to *The Book of Irish Ballads* (Dublin, 1846, 22–3), quoted by D. Lloyd (see note 5 to Introduction here), 88–9.
11. *The English Review* (Deddington, Oxon.: Philip Allen, 2, 3 [February 1992]), 28–9.
12. Foster, 41: see note 24 to Introduction here.
13. Tony Harrison, 'Them & [uz]', in *Selected Poems* (Harmondsworth: Penguin, 1984), 123.
14. Randall interview: see note 54 to Chapter 1.
15. *YP* 312.
16. Thomas MacDonagh, *Literature in Ireland* (as note 18 to Chapter 1 here), 128.
17. Paul Muldoon, *Quoof* (London: Faber & Faber, 1983), 39.
18. Smith, 'The Distance Between' (as note 40 to Chapter 1 here) 35–61.
19. C.C. O'Brien, 'A Slow North-East Wind' (*Listener*, 25 September 1975), 404.

20. Ciaran Carson, 'Escaped from the Massacre?' (*Honest Ulsterman*, 50 [Winter 1975]), 183–6.
21. Edna Longley, *Poetry in the Wars* (Newcastle upon Tyne: Bloodaxe, 1986), 140–69.
22. Robert Welch, *Changing States* (as note 31 to Introduction here), 253.
23. For a discussion of this, see R. Jakobson and S. Rudy, 'Yeats' "Sorrow of Love" Through the Years', in R. Jakobson, *Verbal Art, Verbal Sign, Verbal Time,* (as note 49 to Chapter 1 above), 79–107.
24. C.C. O'Brien, 'Passion and Cunning: An Essay on Yeats's Politics', in *Passion and Cunning and Other Essays* (London: Weidenfeld & Nicolson, 1988), 8–61. Originally published 1965.
25. Dillon Johnston, *Irish Poetry After Joyce* (Notre Dame, IN: University of Notre Dame Press; and Mountrath: The Dolmen Press, 1985), 145.
26. *King Lear*, I, i, 92, in *The Riverside Shakespeare* (as note 34 to chapter 1 above), 1257.
27. YP 302.
28. Seamus Heaney, *Stations* (Belfast: Ulsterman Publications, 1975), 22.
29. James Randall, 'An Interview with Seamus Heaney' (Ploughshares, 5, 3 [1979]), 21.
30. H. Vendler, *The Music of What Happens* (as note 38 to Chapter 1 above), 152.
31. *ibid.*, 156.
32. Neil Corcoran, 'Quickened into Verb' (as note 37 to Introduction above), 69.
33. Osip Mandelstam, *Selected Poems*, trans. Clarence Brown and W.S. Merwin (New York: Atheneum, 1974), 7.
34. W.B. Yeats, *Essays and Introductions*, 522 (as note 11 to Chapter 1 above).
35. Randall interview (as note 29 above), 21.
36. Frank Kinahan, 'Artists on Art: An Interview with Seamus Heaney' (*Critical Inquiry*, 8, 3 [Spring 1982]), 404–14.
37. *ibid.*
38. Roy Foster, *Paddy and Mr Punch* (London: Allen Lane, The Penguin Press, 1993), 288.
39. Curtha i láthair ag Seán Ó Tuama, with translations into English verse by Thomas Kinsella (Portlaoise: The Dolmen Press, 1981).
40. Dante, *Paradiso III*, 85.
41. Helen Vendler, 'Echoes, Soundings, Searches, Probes' (originally published in the *New Yorker*, 23 September 1985), reprinted in H. Bloom (ed.), *Seamus Heaney: Modern Critical Views* (New York: Chelsea House, 1986), 175.

Chapter 3 'The limbo of lost words': The Sweeney Complex

1. Interview with Dennis O'Driscoll, 'Heaney's Sweeney', *Hibernia* (Dublin), 11 October 1979, 13.
2. Flann O'Brien, *At Swim-Two-Birds* (Harmondsworth: Penguin, 1967), 71. Originally published 1939.
3. Quotations from first edition (Derry: Field Day, 1983), 39.
4. See note 50 to Chapter 1 here.
5. 'South Bank Show', 27 October 1991.
6. Heaney's vigorous, vernacular Dante recalls the pre-nineteenth-century view of him as 'Gothic', seeing the adjectives of *Inferno* I, 5 as applicable to his own style: '*selvaggia e aspra e forte*': 'wild and harsh and strong', despite the claims in *De Vulgari Eloquentia* for the 'Cardinal, Courtly and Curial' nature of the Illustrious Vernacular which surpasses all local usages. For 'Envies and Identifications' see note 6 to Chapter 5.
7. T.S. Eliot, *The Complete Poems and Plays of T.S. Eliot* (London: Faber & Faber, 1969), 195.
8. *ibid.*, 193.
9. *YP*, 325.
10. *ibid.*, 322.
11. George Moore, *Hail and Farewell*, ed. Richard Cave (Gerrards Cross, Bucks.: Colin Smythe, 1985), 540. Originally published 1914.
12. 'A Prayer for my Daughter', *YP* 296.
13. *YP* 350.
14. Patrick Kavanagh, 254 (see note 42 to Chapter 1 above).
15. *Honest Ulsterman*, 32 (January/February 1972), 28–9.
16. O'Brien, *At Swim-Two-Birds*, 85 (see note 2 above).
17. *YP* 317.
18. Smith, 'The Distance Between'; see note 40 to Chapter 1, 59.
19. See note 1 above.
20. *The Sunday Times*, 12 June 1988. See note 16 to Chapter 5 below.

Chapter 4 Beyond the Alphabet: *The Haw Lantern* and *Seeing Things*

1. Morrison 53. Vendler says: 'Heaney is the sort of poet who, because he is so accomplished in each stage, is begrudged his new departures; we want more of what so pleased us earlier. (*The Music of What Happens*, 152). See note 30 to Chapter 2 above.
2. Peter Levi's review of *Seeing Things* in *Poetry Review*, 81, 2, (Summer 1991), 12.

3. Michael Allen's review of *The Haw Lantern* in *The Irish Review*, 3; see note 50 to Chapter 1.
4. Smith, 'The Distance Between'; see note 40 to Chapter 1, 53.
5. Allen, ' "Holding Course" '; see note 50 to Chapter 1, 200.
6. Douglas Dunn, *Elegies* (London: Faber & Faber, 1985).
7. *The Cure at Troy* (London: Faber & Faber, 1990).
8. Cf. Alan Robinson, *Instabilities* 137. See note 25 to Introduction above.
9. *ibid.*, 139.
10. *Beowulf*, ll. 26–52. ed. Fr. Klaeber (Boston, MA: D. C. Heath, 1922) 2–3.
11. For the importance of liminality, see, for example, Jacques Derrida's 'Tympan', in *A Derrida Reader: Between the Blinds*, ed. Peggy Karnaf (Hemel Hempstead: Harvester Wheatsheaf, 1991), 146 ff.
12. F. de Saussure, *Course in General Linguistics*, trans. and annotated Roy Harris (London: Duckworth, 1983), 67 ff.
13. YP 325.
14. Giraldus Cambrensis, *History and Topography of Ireland*, trans. J.J. O'Meara (1951; Harmondsworth: Penguin, 1982), 111.
15. D.H. Lawrence, *The Rainbow*, ed. M. Kinkead-Weekes (Cambridge: Cambridge University Press, 1989). Chapter IX, 'The Marsh and the Flood', 230.
16. W.H. Auden, 'Wrapped in a yielding air': line 17 is 'The friendless and unhated stone', which neatly illustrates the openness of negatived forms. Does 'unhated' mean 'liked', or 'viewed with indifference', or something else?
17. Desmond Fennell, see note 4 to Introduction above, p. 9.
18. Allen, see note 50 to Chapter 1 above.
19. Seamus Heaney, *The Tree Clock* (Belfast: The Linen Hall Library, 1990).
20. Psalms 22: 16–17.
21. *Oxford English Dictionary*, 2nd edn (1989) (compact one-volume 1991, 1635): '*rust sb*[3]': (colloq.) back-formation from rusty: "to take . . . the rust of a horse", to become restive'.
22. 'Poet's Chair' (Cambridge, MA: Bow and Arrow Press, 1993).
23. B.M.H. Strang, *A History of English* (London: Methuen, 1970), 39 ff.
24. *Times Literary Supplement*, 22 January 1993.
25. For the application of the speech-act theory in Austin's *How to do Things with Words* (1962), see S.C. Levinson, *Pragmatics* (Cambridge: Cambridge University Press, 1983) 228 ff.
26. W.B. Yeats, *Essays and Introductions* (London: Macmillan, 1961), 524.

Chapter 5 Heaney's *ars poetica*: Mandelstam, Dante and *The Government of the Tongue*

1. This comment was made by Edward Mendelson in his *Times Literary Supplement* review (1–7 July 1988), 726.
2. First as 'The Interesting Case of John Alphonsus Mulrennan' in *Planet*, January 1978, 34–40, taking its title from the sympathetic parochial philosopher at the end of Joyce's *A Portrait of the Artist as a Young Man* (Harmondsworth: Penguin, 1992), 274. See Seamus Deane's note 271 in that edition, p. 329. This was adapted as a lecture to the Royal Dublin Society in 1986, and published in *Shenandoah* as 'The Interesting Case of Nero, Chekhov's Cognac and a Knocker', the title under which it appears in *The Government of the Tongue*.
3. For this point, see Jamie McKendrick's review, 'Poetry's Governing Power', in *Poetry Durham*, 20 (Winter 1988/89), 34–8.
4. 'Conversation about Dante', trans. Jane Gary Harris, is conveniently available in Osip Mandelstam, *The Collected Critical Prose and Letters*, ed. J.G. Harris (London: Collins Harvill, 1991), 397–442. Hereafter 'Mandelstam CP'.
5. See Neil Corcoran, 'Seamus Heaney and the Art of the Exemplary' as in note 5 to Chapter 1 above, 117–27.
6. 'Envies and Identifications: Dante and the Modern Poet' (*Irish University Review*, 15, 1 [Spring 1985]), 5–19.
7. *YP* 264.
8. 'Envies and Identifications', 9–10.
9. Mandelstam CP, 678.
10. The first line of the canto wishes for '*rime aspre e chiocche*' ('harsh and grating verses') to describe the darkest bottom of Hell, where Ugolino and Archbishop Ruggieri, who make such an impression on Heaney, are found.
11. Mandelstam CP, 430.
12. *ibid.*, 430–1.
13. *ibid.*, 123–4. See note 33 to Chapter 2 for Brown and Merwin versions of Mandelstam.
14. In Paul de Man, *The Resistance to Theory* (Manchester: Manchester University Press, 1986), 21–6.
15. Mandelstam CP, 313, in the 'Fourth Prose'.
16. Carey says aphoristically: 'Heaney's whole poetic input could be seen as a hymn to doubt' (*The Sunday Times*, 12 June 1988).
17. This tends to be even more true in Part II of *GT*, which comprises the University of Kent T.S. Eliot Lectures themselves. Eliot receives a higher profile there – naturally enough, given the occasion's aegis.

But we should be wary of the apparent statistical dominance of Eliot. By my count there are at least twenty-six explicit references to Eliot in *GT*, which is far more than to Dante, for example; but this does not necessarily mean that Dante is less important in Heaney's poetic.

18. *Times Literary Supplement*, 31 October 1980. Reprinted as 'The Hiding Places of Power' in Bloom, 124.
19. The phrase comes from 'A Snowshoe', Part 6 of Heaney's sequence 'Shelf Life' in *Station Island* (*SI* 24).
20. 'The Ways of the Possible. A Textual Analysis of "Gifts of Rain" by Seamus Heaney', in *Studies in Seamus Heaney*, ed. Jacqueline Genet (Centre de Publication de l'Université de Caen, 1987), 27–45.
21. See note 39 to Introduction here.
22. Ezra Pound's translation of 'Donna mi prega' is a remarkably enlightening interpretation of this notoriously difficult poem. See *The Translations of Ezra Pound* (London: Faber & Faber, 1953), 132–41.
23. *Harpers and Queen* (December 1988), 42.
24. See note 1 to Introduction here.
25. *Cencrastus* (Autumn 1988), 51.
26. *Spectator* (5 November 1988), vol. 261, no. 8365, 46.
27. The Dublin *Sunday Independent* (10 July 1988).
28. See Chapter 3, note 6; note 10 to this Chapter above.
29. See note 1 to Chapter 3 here.
30. *Purgatorio* XXIV, 52–4.
31. 'Like sap at the end of green sticks on a fire' draws on the simile in *Inferno* XIII, 40 ff., which compares the voice that issues from a speaking tree (a decidedly Heaneyesque notion) to the sound made by the sap boiling from a burning green stick.

Bibliography

Since a full bibliography is currently being prepared by Randy Brandes, and should appear at roughly the same time as this book, this is a very select list, confined to Heaney's major publications and full-length books on him, whether unitary critical studies or anthologies of critical essays. I have not included the interim volumes of poems, and I have made no attempt to itemise the reviews and articles in journals. Neither have I included here those individual essays and reviews on which I have drawn in the body of the text; they are referenced in the notes and index, and it would be pointlessly selective to distinguish them from the full range of such writings. Finally, I have not listed works by writers other than Heaney, even those cited frequently, such as Yeats's poems. Such works can be traced from the index, referenced in full at first occurrence.

1. Works by Seamus Heaney

All published in London by Faber & Faber, unless the contrary is specified.

Death of a Naturalist (1966).
Door into the Dark (1969).
Wintering Out (1972).
Stations (Belfast: Ulsterman Publications, 1975).

North (1975).

Field Work (1979).

Selected Poems 1965–1975 (1980).

Preoccupations: Selected Prose 1968–1978 (1980).

An Open Letter (Derry: Field Day Theatre Company, 1983).

Sweeney Astray (Derry: Field Day Theatre Company, 1983 and London: Faber & Faber, 1984).

Station Island (1984).

The Haw Lantern (1987).

The Government of the Tongue; The 1986 T.S. Eliot Memorial Lectures and Other Critical Writings (1988).

The Cure at Troy: A Version of Sophocles' Philoctetes (Derry: Field Day Theatre Company, 1990).

Seeing Things (1991).

The Midnight Verdict (Oldcastle: The Gallery Press, 1994).

2. Writings on Seamus Heaney

Andrews, Elmer. *The Poetry of Seamus Heaney: All the Realms of Whisper* (London: Macmillan, 1988).

Andrews, Elmer (ed.), *Seamus Heaney: A Collection of Critical Essays* (London: Macmillan, 1992).

Bloom, Harold (ed.), *Seamus Heaney: Modern Critical Views* (New York: Chelsea House, 1986).

Buttel, Robert. *Seamus Heaney* (Lewisburg: Bucknell University Press, 1975).

Corcoran, Neil. *Seamus Heaney* (London: Faber, 1986).

Curtis, Tony. *The Art of Seamus Heaney* (Bridgend: Poetry Wales Press, 1982). The revised second edition (1985) is the one I have used here. The further revised third edition is to be published in 1994.

Foster, Thomas C. *Seamus Heaney* (Dublin: The O'Brien Press, 1989).

Hart, Henry. *Seamus Heaney: Poet of Contrary Progressions* (New York: Syracuse University Press, 1992).

Morrison, Blake. *Seamus Heaney* (London: Methuen, 1982).

Tamplin, Ronald. *Seamus Heaney* (Milton Keynes: Open University Press, 1989).

Parker, Michael. *Seamus Heaney: The Making of the Poet* (Dublin: Gill & Macmillan, 1993).

Index

The Index refers to all names that occur in the book and the Notes, as well as to major topics. I have indexed book references in the Notes only on their first occurrence; thereafter they are cross-referred to in the Notes themselves.